"The title, 'From Bullied to Brilliant' says it all. It's all about resilience and becoming the best person that you can be. It's about moving on through the pitfalls of life. I love the positive nature of the messages in this book and Karen's own positive outlook on life and raising children is clearly evident.
The combination of referring back to the great philosophies through the ages and, as Karen calls it, some 'uncommon sense', provides valuable insights for parents struggling with how to help their children work through situations of bullying and intimidation. The strategies are sound and a breath of fresh air. I have helped young people deal with bullying issues for over 36 years and associate very closely with Karen's peaceful, non-judgmental approach. A must-read for parents and educators which should be shared with your children."

Chris Gold
Principal of St John's College
Australia

"As a parent, grandparent and educator I commend this book. Much has been discussed around the subject of bullying and all too often, there is an emphasis on the victim. If this problem is to be truly explored, we must take a look at the bully. This will give those affected by bullying an insight into the mind of the bully and furnish them with the necessary tools to be placed in a position of understanding and power. In 'From Bullied to Brilliant' Karen takes an holistic view, bringing a refreshing and rounded approach to this growing problem.
Well done Karen!"

Christine Hall
Education Consultant
United Kingdom

"The people who are different, eccentric, who don't fit the mould - are the people who, because of their non-conformity, have the ability to think outside the box and do things differently. Unfortunately, this asset also makes them a target. 'From Bullied to Brilliant' is a wonderful tool to help those people both understand and deal with bullies, and embrace their own potential for brilliance."

Matthew Mitcham
Olympian
www.twistsandturns.com.au
Australia

"I was born during World War 2, when unchecked bullying produced two psychotic mass murderers, Hitler and Stalin, who slaughtered 50 million people. They were empowered by compliant, obedient citizens who invested their own life-force in the bullies; pleading 'I was only following orders'. Later in life I met a psychologist, Dr John Bieshon, who dealt with bullying at work. He brought the bullies, the victims, their colleagues and managers together and to their senses. He accentuated the positive to eliminate the negative to make the organisation and the world a better place. Those were adults, whose psyches were formed and fixed. Karen's important book shines bold, bright clear light into the dark corners where bullying and fearful compliance take root and grow, in families, nurseries, schools, recreations and relationships. And she guides us on how to intelligently confront the syndrome as early as possible, to counter it and liberate all the players to enjoy their lives. Karen's greatest gift to her readers is her exemplary courage in revealing her own battles and vulnerabilities. This is not a Do As I Say – but a creative Do As I Do book - from which we may all draw inspiration, courage, wisdom and strength."

Noel Hodson, Author
AD 2516 - After Global Warming
www.noelhodson.com
United Kingdom

"I have worked with Karen in children's workshops over several years, and I have watched 'From Bullied to Brilliant' grow from strategies based on her own experiences to a concept that can change a worldwide pattern of bullying. The book Karen has created is easy to understand and use for teachers, students, bullies and victims. I am so proud to have been close enough to watch the book grow and next I will watch it change the world."

Hayley Green
Director
Ausfunkpower Dance and Self Confidence Workshops
Co-Founder Own 2 Feet
www.ausfunk.com.au
Australia

"Those of us who are dreamers and misfits often find ourselves with a bulls-eye painted on our backs. We can feel like our uniqueness is something to be ashamed of, rather than a gift to be embraced. 'From Bullied to Brilliant' helps those of us who have been through, are going through, or may one day experience bullying - and sends the important message that we are not alone by sharing encouraging stories from those who have made it through to the other side."

Ed Francis
Executive Director/Co-Founder, Rhythm Workshops
Master Drum Coach/Founder, Round Rock Drums
www.roundrockdrums.com
www.rhythmworkshops.org
United States of America

"I loved reading 'From Bullied to Brilliant' for both personal and business reasons.
Personally as someone who allowed myself to be bullied until my mid-30s, the book was a wonderful confirmation of just how far I have come, especially in regards to taking responsibility of my own world. I won't lie to you; the book triggered several past emotions and, a few regrets that it had not been published 20 years earlier. It was very much worth the journey though.
As a counsellor I found myself reading the book from a therapeutic perspective. 'From Bullied to Brilliant' contains many gems for anyone who works with bullied clients. I believe it to be a must-have for those who work with children, including teachers. The book goes beyond what we learn in the textbooks or what we see on the surface. The sharing of stories gives us a deeper look into the world of the bullied and the bully. Maybe if we could gain a deeper understanding to pass on to our children at an early age, some future trauma could be avoided.
What I particularly loved was the lack of judgment, the practical tools for all parties, the compassion for all sides, and the allowed space for healing."

Kama Frankling
Slow Down and Play Therapist
www.almoststressfree.com
United Kingdom

"'From Bullied to Brilliant' offers deep-reaching strategies and techniques for overcoming bullying. The book provides great insight and understanding into a world which is too often swept under the carpet or dealt with behind closed doors. In a corporate environment, bullying is an important issue in ethics policy. As such, this book not only offers individuals solutions, it also offers corporations relevant and realistic tools to help deal with those being bullied, as well as those doing the bullying.

Rachael Handley (MSc, PGCE)
Corporate Training Manager
Dubai

"I am fortunate to be able to say that I and those around me have never experienced the situations highlighted in 'From Bullied to Brilliant' and despite that, Karen has educated me with informative, thought provoking and practical examples of what to do when faced with bullying. As a grandfather, I want all my children to read this book and discuss it with their children. It should become a standard reference for those seeking to understand and contend with a scourge that is all too prevalent in today's society."

Mark Wyatt
State Manager AA Radio Services Pty Ltd.
Dad of 5 and Poppy of 4
Australia

"Karen Clarke takes a clear look at bullying and presents her message in a straight talking, practical yet compassionate way. She tells it like she sees it, and through her honesty and empathy, she hands over the keys of healing to anyone who has experienced bullying first hand, or knows someone who is experiencing bullying. Two of the many empowering messages in 'From Bullied to Brilliant' are that bullying is not a new phenomenon – it's been part of the social and human experience since time immemorial – only the shape it takes has changed in some instances. The other is that anyone can handle a bullying situation, no matter how 'weak' or submissive they see themselves as being. With a firm hand and an open heart, Karen Clarke walks with you through this clear sighted and courageous book."

Jill Chivers
Conscious Consumption Writer and Advocate
www.jillchivers.com
Australia

"Bullying has long been thought of as a necessary evil in one form or another. Here at last is an intelligent investigation that not only explains the phenomenon and gives some real life examples but also suggests practical measures to overcome the problem.
Written with wit and a heartfelt desire to make a difference, Karen Clarke shows that there are solutions that can be life changing, leading to a positive and joyful outcome. A book that is most definitely worth reading."

Sylvia Hodson
Professeur
L'université Aix/Marseille
France

This book is dedicated to those who choose to be brilliant
and shine light on this weary world.
I salute you.

FROM BULLIED
TO *Brilliant*

How to artfully avoid fitting in

Karen Clarke

www.frombulliedtobrilliant.com

admin@frombulliedtobrilliant.com

Editing by: Alex Mitchell www.AuthorSupportServices.com

Cover design by: Jeanne Treloar www.SassyBranding.com.au

Illustrations by: Susie Baxter-Smith susiesmith1@optusnet.com.au

Proofreading by: Julia Gibbs www.juliaproofreader.wordpress.com

Geoffrey David West www.geoffreydavidwest.com

Designed, Printed and Bound in Australia by: InHouse Publishing

National Library of Australia Cataloguing-in-Publication

Author: Clarke, Karen, author.

Title: From bullied to brilliant: how to artfully avoid fitting in/Karen Clarke.

ISBN: 9780987564801 (paperback)

Subjects: Bullying.

Bullying--Prevention.

Children--Life skills guides.

Dewey Number: 371.58

Published by Karen Clarke and Inhouse Publishing www.inhousepublishing.com.au

Acknowledgements

"If I have seen further than others, it is by standing upon the shoulders of giants"

Isaac Newton

Firstly, I would like to offer a word of thanks to the people who have been instrumental in the creation of this body of work. For those late night Skypes and early morning read-throughs, to all who have contributed ideas, stories, quotes, inspiration and support, moral or otherwise, and whose material I have referenced, I am eternally and unequivocally grateful. Amongst these special thanks go to Principal of St John's College Chris Gold, and Education Consultant Christine Hall, also Noel Hodson, Kama Frankling, Hayley Green and Sue Murphy for going above and beyond the call

Thank you to the many people who have helped turn my vision into a physical reality, including, amongst many others, Alex Mitchell whose commitment as an editor has been truly commendable, Zoe Wyatt, Mark Wyatt, Dr. Steve Gration (B.Ed PhD), Jeanne Treloar, Susie Baxter-Smith, Vanessa Webster, Ocean Reeve, Jill Chivers, Julia Gibbs and Geoffrey David West.

Special thanks to the wonderful contributors: Ed Francis, Matthew Mitcham, Michael Schwandt, Tanja Mitton, Alison Laverty, Yvette Adams and of course those who wish to remain anonymous. Your stories are the fabric that binds this book together and I am deeply indebted to each and every one of you. Special thanks also to our wonderful *From Bullied to Brilliant* coaches Natalie Hennessey and Tracey Carmichael for your superb words of wisdom, your amazing depth of knowledge and your loving support of this vision.

I would also like to express my deepest gratitude to Dr. Arun Gandhi for his willingness to write a foreword for my humble book. I am both honoured and blessed. Your tireless dedication to sharing Mahatma Gandhi's message of non-violent resistance is much needed in a world that is crying out for solutions. A million times, thank you.

To my dear, loyal, trusting and beautiful friends, who continue to inspire me. You know who you are, and I will not forget.

My deep thanks also go to Sylvia, who has remained supportive, loving, steady and comforting when I doubted that it was all indeed worthwhile. You are the best of mothers and I am so very grateful that you are mine.

I would like to thank my wonderful husband Wayne who generously shared his knowledge and experience in this field. Without his love, support, inspiration and never-ending conveyor belt of toast, tea and delicious meals, this book would never have come to fruition, and remained a whim, lost forever in the ether. Our personal experiences with bullying and intimidation are very different; however our willingness, ability and unwavering enthusiasm to overcome these challenges have many similarities. Without his input, I would not have formed the same conclusions or been able to articulate this message effectively. Thank you Wayne for your ever-present love and support. You are and always will be the love of my life.

Last but not least I would like to thank my three children, Isaac, Mayah and Elias for your tolerance, support, wisdom, kindness and love. You have been my research source, my guinea pigs, my inspiration and my guides. You made this dream a reality and I love you.

Contributors

Ed Francis

Michael Schwandt

Amanda

Ryan

Yvette Adams

Alison Laverty

Tanja Mitton

Matthew Mitcham

Tracey Carmichael

Natalie Hennessey

Foreword

Dr. Arun Gandhi

Bullying is an inexorable part of the culture of violence that dominates human society. We tend to blame young men and women as irresponsible, evil and inconsiderate because they terrify their colleagues in schools. But they are actually acting out what they see in adult societies.

After all, when you think of it everyone today is a bully of sorts. Parents bully their children, siblings bully each other, employers bully employees, governments bully citizens and so life in a culture of violence goes on. It is only the degree and depth of the bullying that ultimately changes. Every time we intentionally intimidate someone into doing our bidding it is bullying.

In the past, the culture of violence existed but was not as overpowering as it is today. The culture of violence assumed a more intense and frightening image over the last hundred years—especially since World War II. Until WWII, violence was contained and controlled. Now violence has no limits. It pervades our sports, entertainment, business, religion, relationships; in short our entire life is violent. Often it seems as though people in power and authority are determined to brainwash citizens, starting with children as young as possible, into accepting violence as a natural way of life. More and more games are invented to induce children into thinking that fighting, killing and maiming is a fun activity. Parents spend precious money to buy these violent video games for their children in the belief that their children will learn to protect themselves in a world that is becoming more berserk by the day. We are, in fact, making our children immune to violence and bloodshed.

Added to this mix is the proliferating weapons industry that has to sell the products it makes. So it creates citizens' organisations like the National Rifle Association to promote the sale and possession of weapons of mass destruction as a human right. The Bible clearly says: 'Those who live by the sword shall die by the sword'. But then, the words of the Bible are meant to be uttered only on Sundays in church. Then the Bible and Jesus are locked up for the next six days.

If violence is fascinating and human life is cheap, why are we so concerned when some people act out in our schools and streets? If we are willing to allow violence to dominate our lives, we should be prepared to accept the consequences.

Tomes will be written on the subject of eliminating bullying but it will make little difference until we, as awakened human beings, are willing to open our eyes to the evils of violence and contain it. Experts say that what a child experiences during the first five or six years of their life determines the child's fate. In modern societies homes are wrecked, marriages break up and parents become bullies in the name of disciplining their children. When a child experiences these negative emotions and actions at home they learn to use the same tactics to intimidate someone they can dominate. The behaviour of a child is a clear indicator of the kind of home the child comes from. Bullies come from homes where parents bully their children.

It is not for nothing that people like Grandfather Gandhi said, "We must become the change we wish to see in the world". Unless we adults are able to check and control our fascination with violence and gradually transform the culture of violence into a culture of nonviolence, bullying is going to be a part of childhood and nothing is going to control it. The cancer that creates the bullying and eats away at our body politic cannot be cured by Band-Aid therapy. It needs radical surgery. Bullying is deeply embedded in our historical and cultural story and will remain until we address the underlying problems. Karen's book opens the door to the wisdom of Gandhi and will help to the extent that one is willing to change drastically in behaviour and thinking. *From Bullied to Brilliant* leads to a greater understanding of the mechanisms which engender and encourage bullying and contains valuable strategies and tools for overcoming these very problems.

To those who believe that violence is the only way for humanity to survive and live, they may, unfortunately, discover that contentment, fulfilment and peace remain forever an elusive dream.

Arun Gandhi
President, Gandhi Worldwide Education Institute, USA
Leader of the Gandhi Legacy Tour of India.
www.gandhiforchildren.org
www.gandhitour.info

Preface

*"Let him that would move
the world first move himself"*

Socrates

Why is this book different? Primarily it is because the concepts to support people who are facing bullying and intimidation, have been written as a result of both professional and profoundly painful personal experience. It is my belief that we need to add some creative thinking to the current conventional wisdom. We need to instil some uncommon sense into a domain that has largely been ignored as a serious problem, and in which many of the tools and techniques we are encouraged to use, simply don't work. The world needs a little more *oomph* to overcome and move beyond bullying.

Both this book and my coaching practice support parents and their children to find immediate, practical solutions to the bullying problem. Also, I have three primary and high-school aged children, which positions me at the pointy end of the bullying stick and offers daily reminders of the issues facing young people. The solutions I have discovered have largely not been a result of the current systems we have in place, ergo the systems have room for improvement and consequently, room for this book.

When focusing on problems associated with bullying and intimidation, I know *exactly* what it's like to feel embarrassed, isolated, insecure and alone. I was aggressively ostracised by my peer group in primary school, teased mercilessly throughout my early years and moved to West Africa aged 15, where I experienced a hellish year in a hot, humid and hostile French-speaking school. I grew up as the only girl in a family of seven children, feeling shy, gangly, gauche, unattractive, physically inept and insignificant. I know distinctly what it feels like to not fit in, to feel rejected, unwanted, unimportant and lacking in personal power. Perhaps ironically, I also have known what it feels like inadvertently to bully, or to hurt others. If we were all truly honest with ourselves, haven't we all at some point caused another pain, either intentionally or otherwise?

Thankfully I have managed to move well beyond the uncomfortable sleep of victimhood and the never-ending spiral of hurt that accompanies it.

Through my work I have been fortunate enough to assist many parents or carers and children to move beyond the bully/victim cycle, and as a result have pinpointed key elements that speed up the process and help people move into their natural and intrinsic state of confidence and self-esteem. My training, professional expertise and life experience have provided me with unique and valuable tools which help me understand *how* to shift focus from the problem to a very immediate solution and, if you are willing to read on and take action, so will you.

As you will learn through this journey, I also have a clear understanding of how it feels to *be under the impression* that you are isolated, bullied and without support. I hope that, through the sharing of these stories and the offering of transformative steps to confidence and self-esteem, you will see that you are truly not alone, never were, never will be. You will learn that many, many great people throughout history and in the present day have walked in your shoes, been used and abused by friend and enemy alike, and used their hardship and in some cases severe trauma and pain as a springboard to boost them in the direction of their dreams.

"Listen to everything, forget much, correct little."

Pope John XXIII

Contents

Introduction

*"I have nothing new to teach the world. Truth and non-violence
are as old as the hills. All I have done is to try experiments in both
on as vast a scale as I could"*

Mahatma Gandhi

From Bullied to Brilliant is intended to ease the hurt of people who are experiencing intimidation, aggression, and bullying or have fallen into the unpleasant, unnecessary and slippery trap of feeling unworthy or low in confidence and self-esteem. It is also of value to those who are experiencing themselves as bullies, for absolutely the same reasons.

When I began writing, my original intention was to create something for the parents of children experiencing bullying at school and something for the clients of my coaching practice, who needed support and encouragement to find their way out of the bullying cycle. What I didn't realise at the time is that you don't so much write a book as bring it to life. It emerges almost randomly out of the data swirling around your head and the intuitions in your heart. Ultimately, it writes you. As such, I have realised that this collection of words is instead a guide for people who are like me, or perhaps like the 15-year-old version of me that existed before I began my journey of discovery to find the elusive confidence and self-esteem that 'other people' appeared to have.

This is a book for people who either know what it feels like to be bullied and intimidated or would like to help or support someone who is struggling with low confidence and self-esteem. It is a guide for people who find it easy to believe in their lack of worth and value in the world and who find it easy to see themselves as unimportant and incompetent. It is for people who struggle with a self-image that is painful and uncomfortable and are either facing or creating bullying. They may well find themselves helplessly observing their own children experiencing similar problems. If any of this sounds familiar, this book is for you.

I am not a psychologist or psychiatrist, do not hold a Master's degree in any domain, do not have a degree or PhD. My professional coaching training is in NLP, Time Line Therapy® and hypnosis. My coaching clinic in Australia specialises in the support of individuals and families affected by bullying and, thanks to the internet, is available worldwide. My personal experience is diverse and richly peppered with exotic travel, cultural and emotional challenges, spanning from the Pennines in the north of England to tropical West Africa, France, New Zealand and Australia.

Much of what you are about to read is an intermingling of personal and professional life experience. Most importantly, it is about real life bullying, intimidation and abuse, includes references to my journey and that of many others, and explores the complications that arise for people who feel victimised, isolated and ostracised.

In order to fully comprehend bullying we need to recognise that, in addition to schoolyard and workplace bullying, corporal punishment, abuse, domestic violence, and war are all part of the same story. Violence is violence, domination is domination, bullying and abuse are bullying and abuse. The only thing that changes is the setting.

Here you will learn not only how to overcome bullying and intimidation but also how to find yourself in the process. You will understand how feeling bullied and intimidated are states of mind, and will discover how to make changes so that the *feeling* of intimidation is no longer a key driver in your life. Within these pages we will also look at understanding bullying in a broader, deeper and perhaps more compassionate sense. Bullies are victims who lash out, victims are people who bully themselves.

You will find information and suggestions to understand the bully/victim cycle in a deeper sense; what it is, why it happens, how it happens and how it manifests in our modern world. We will look at the many faces of bullying and create a rich appreciation of how and why bullying causes such problems for so many people. You will also find suggestions and tips to help transition through this cycle.

If you are a parent or teacher helping a child or student, you will be able to read and share this information together. Through this process, both of you can discover a deeper and more realistic understanding of bullying and as a result develop your own plans, strategies and systems.

I will share a systemised approach to personal power, confidence and self-esteem as a tangible, easy-to-implement and effective formula that facilitates the rapid transformation *From Bullied to Brilliant*. It is my wish that the information contained within these pages will help you move out of feelings of isolation and despair to feelings of resourcefulness and personal power. It is my deepest desire that this book plays a significant role in ending the bully/victim cycle that plagues our planet so that we may evolve into more creative and life-enhancing practices.

The life and teachings of Mohandas Gandhi are the primary inspiration for this work, and his unwavering devotion to non-violent resistance and deep love of humanity is at the very core of my message. The seven step acronym **B-Gandhi** is in honour of his life changing, peace loving contribution to the world.

If you are hurting, and you are scared, please realise that as painful as it may be, you are NOT and never will be, alone.

"You must not lose faith in humanity. Humanity is an ocean; if a few drops of the ocean are dirty, the ocean does not become dirty"

Mahatma Gandhi

FROM BULLIED TO *Brilliant*

SECTION 1

UNDERSTANDING BULLYING

*"First they ignore you, then they laugh at you,
then they fight you, then you win"*

Mohandas Gandhi

Bullying is a controversial topic which mobilises parents and stirs up deep emotions. Due to the increased proliferation of technology and ready access to media, it is becoming an increasingly *observable* problem across the globe but not necessarily an increasing problem. It is however a commanding buzzword amongst education and workplace authorities, and now, adding much glamour to the issue, notable celebrities are passionately joining the furore. Some parents of children entering the school system find themselves acutely fearful of the threat that the school playground offers, and are at a loss when a serious incident occurs.

Families with high-school aged children who have not as yet developed strong social skills, or are not particularly resilient in the face of criticism or ridicule, feel anxious and helpless as they witness their young progeny launch themselves into the abyss of semi-adult life, unskilled and unprepared for the challenges they face. Instead of experiencing a thrill of anticipation as they witness their cherished offspring expand and grow into adult independence, some parents feel a bit like they have thrown their vulnerable charge to the wolves.

There are also parents whose children are destined to bully, children whose preferred negotiation tool is dominance and control and who have little or no recourse to stop their child from facing a school life fraught with drama and intervention. Workplace managers and educators are facing challenges related to bullying with an equal amount of alarm and an equal lack of effective tools.

Our world has still not discovered that bullying is a futile and meaningless search for dominance and control of others. Frustratingly, humanity is stuck in a recurring cycle as bullying is still undeniably present in schools, workplaces, politics both national and international, within relationships and across societies and cultures.

However, are we as powerless to control this problem as it seems? Is it really becoming more of a problem or have many people simply forgotten their innate ability to manage emotional balance effectively? Do we now live in a world bereft of common sense? Is the illusion that people *should* behave nicely towards us, *should* be kind, tolerant and respectful in fact limiting our potential to feel special, empowered and independent or just plain good about ourselves? Is it true that in order for us to feel powerful, creative, confident and loved, others *must* support us and lift us up? Or is this thought an illusion? Are we in truth all able to access the same resources, self-belief and personal power that drives accomplished and successful people to achieve results? If that is so, how do we do it?

"You can never cross the ocean unless you have the courage to lose sight of the shore"

Christopher Columbus

Perhaps our problem lies not in the fact that bullies exist in the world, but in our willingness to hand over our personal power and become despondent, miserable and defenceless when faced with opposition. It may be rather confronting to acknowledge that we are willing to experience ourselves as victims but there is a great deal of evidence to support the idea that we each indeed do hold the key to our own happiness, and that regardless of our circumstances, we all have within us the unquenchable, untouchable and unstoppable ability to lead fulfilled and joyful lives.

Through my research, and personal and professional experience, I have noticed that confidence and a sense of personal power and self-esteem are essential ingredients in the formula required to transcend the bullying cycle. Devoting time to cultivating confidence and self-esteem leads to happier, more fulfilled and creative lives. Put simply, if you feel good about yourself, you worry less about the negativity around you and will focus instead on your goals and aspirations. Other people's negative behaviours become less overwhelming and difficult to deal with and you move back into your personal power as your attention inevitably moves on to more important matters.

What does personal power mean exactly? It means you shift your focus from the problem to the solution. You become the driver instead of a passenger on this journey we call life. It means you claim back your ability to face and overcome difficulties, challenges and obstacles. It means you remember who you really are at the core and express that without fear or censure.

In order to achieve personal power you need to focus inward, become *self-centred,* and in doing so are better able to tap into your unique gifts, which will in turn help you become more loving, joyful, compassionate and valuable to others. You live pro-actively instead of reactively, become balanced, inwardly strong, creative and better able to form healthy and loving relationships as opposed to needs-based, dependent relationships.

In short, you redress the bully/ victim cycle by tapping into the resources and tools you have at your disposal and consequently you are able to lead a more balanced, happy and fulfilled life.

"To keep our faces toward change and behave like free spirits in the presence of fate is strength undefeatable"

Helen Keller

What is a Bully?

"Be kind, for everyone you meet is fighting a hard battle"

Plato

Oxford Dictionary:
*Noun—**bully** – a person who uses strength or influence to harm or intimidate those who are weaker.*
*Verb—**bullies, bullying, bullied** – use superior strength or influence to intimidate (someone), typically to force them to do something.*

Before we grab our pitchforks and begin demonising and tearing down those in our community who demonstrate bullying behaviour, let's make one thing clear. A fundamental premise of this method of examining and overcoming problems is that you accept (temporarily if you must) the idea that a person is NOT their behaviour. Behaviour itself is fluid, adaptable and changeable. What is perceived as bullying by one person is not necessarily considered bullying by another. Many a bully has been surprised to discover that their actions have caused another pain.

When discussing actual bullying and bullies, we also need to be aware that all people are capable of change and therefore the seeds of compassion, forgiveness and love need to remain alive and present in all of us. A bully is only a bully while they choose to remain so or while they are lost in their own personal story of drama and pain. The minute they change their behaviour they are able to reveal aspects of themselves that have been hidden.

"Within every perceived monster is a wounded angel"

It is also important to note that bullying takes on many faces and presents in many forms. Sometimes it is not dominant and aggressive behaviour, but a very different subtle bullying that can be difficult to detect by anyone other than the victim. This kind of bullying is instigated quietly and without fanfare, is insidious in nature and equally painful to experience.

Overt and Covert Bullying

Overt bullying is where repeated physical actions such as kicking, pushing or punching or verbal actions such as name-calling or insults occur.

Covert bullying is aggressive behaviour which is hidden but is repeated and intended to cause harm. It includes the spreading of rumours or social exclusion, as well as passive-aggressive behaviours such as withholding friendship or affection. Cyber bullying, through the use of technology, emails, mobile phones, social media etc. is a means by which covert bullying can occur.

Covert bullying is intended to cause damage to a person's social reputation and peer relationships, and erode confidence and self-esteem. It is by far the more prevalent problem in schools today, primarily due to our increased social awareness and rejection of physical violence.

Is it Bullying?

How do you know a bully is bullying you? How can you be certain that their behaviour is not perfectly acceptable to them and that it has no real malice or meanness? This raises the issue of *perception,* which bears thinking about if you wish to take control of your thinking and your interpretation of the world around you.

A bully could be described by some or all of the following: a person who is unreasonably and irrationally antagonistic and aggressive; whose intention is to demonstrate power over another through belittling, isolating or subjugating, who behaves in a way that is *intended* to be hurtful and/or cause suffering either through physical, psychological or verbal means. A bully could be a complete stranger, someone in your school or workplace or someone close to you. They could be your parent, child, partner, schoolteacher, manager, co-worker, competitor, sibling or friend.

Bullying can be ascribed to all 'power over' behaviours including but not limited to: domestic abuse, child abuse, corporal punishment, violent acts, rape, prejudice, ostracism or social rejection, teasing, belittling or demeaning others, racism, homophobia, condemnation, bigotry and war.

Conflict or arguments between equals and single incidents are not defined as bullying. Children not getting along well, or a single episode of nastiness, aggression or intimidation also does not constitute bullying.

A bully is NOT an annoying sister/brother who drives you to distraction or a parent imposing seemingly unreasonable house rules. There are many behaviours that occur within families which are part of normal human experience. Siblings will often compete for their parents' attention which can lead to pettiness, sniping, arguing, meanness and in some instances minor (or not so minor) physical contact. Parents, for the smooth running of the home and to teach their children independence and personal discipline, often enforce housekeeping agreements that prove deeply unpopular. Frazzled parents lose their tempers and throw major tantrums from time to time, which can be expected as part of the challenge of living together in close confines. If your family has a system of accountability and is in the habit of acknowledging and apologising for bad behaviour, is able to learn from conflict situations and discuss them freely and openly, then you do not face bullying at home.

It only becomes bullying when the balance is tipped, the conflict becomes largely initiated by one party and causes ongoing, unresolved pain and suffering. Interestingly, within families it is often not the biggest or strongest member of the family who creates the problem.

"I object to violence because when it appears to do good, the good is only temporary; the evil it does is permanent"

Mohandas Gandhi

Bullying behaviours are acutely painful and unreasonable and they far outstrip the usual and healthy negotiation and interplay that occurs in all relationships. They are unexpected, unwelcomed, challenging in the extreme and create suffering as opposed to the normal tensions and frustrations that occur naturally between individuals or groups. If your brother or sister calls you stupid, that does not make him/her a bully. If they *relentlessly* call you stupid without apology or acknowledgment of the impact this behaviour has, some action needs to take place to end the cycle of abuse.

Bullying may include:

- ❀ Physical: hitting, punching, kicking, scratching, tripping, spitting
- ❀ Verbal: name-calling, teasing, putdowns, sarcasm, insults, threats
- ❀ Social: ignoring, excluding, ostracising, alienating
- ❀ Psychological: rumour spreading, dirty looks, hiding or damaging possessions, malicious messaging, inappropriate use of camera phones

There are *no* circumstances where it is acceptable for a child or adult to endure physical violence, mild or otherwise, that is intended for the purpose of domination or subjugation. This includes pushing, shoving and slapping. Domination using physical force is a base animalistic behaviour lacking not only in wisdom, intelligence, intuition, maturity and resourcefulness but also skill, creativity and sensitivity.

The techniques and strategies shared in these pages are valuable in all cases of bullying; however when physical violence is present, I firmly believe that no strategy can successfully bring about lasting change until the violence or threat of violence has been removed.

Violence is the preferred method for those who have not figured out a better way to resolve and solve problems. This applies equally to children in the playground as it does to governments waging wars and politicians spouting 'pre-emptive strikes'. Violence is unacceptable in a world of educated, evolved and intuitive human beings. Evidently as a species, we still have a fair way to go.

"Violence is the last resort of the incompetent"

Isaac Asimov

Bullied is the New Black

"It is in the character of very few men to honour without envy a friend who has prospered"

Aeschylus

As we further explore the murky waters of bullying and abuse, we discover an intriguing paradox. The following list is a compilation of some notable figures who have in their lifetimes experienced bullying. It demonstrates compellingly that bullying occurs regardless of your talent, value, intelligence, skill or ability. If you have been bullied or are being bullied, you are in great company.

Dalai Lama	*Sandra Bullock*	*Chester Bennington*
Mahatma Gandhi	*Howard Stern*	*Jennifer Freeman*
Martin Luther King Jr.	*Miley Cyrus*	*Rose McGowan*
John F. Kennedy	*Michael Phelps*	*Tyra Banks*
Winston Churchill	*Chris Rock*	*Eva Mendes*
Jesus Christ	*Pierce Brosnan*	*Kristen Kruek*
Victor Frankl	*Bill Clinton*	*Hayley Williams*
Elvis Presley	*Tiger Woods*	*Brian McFadden*
Ruby Rose	*Demi Lovato*	*Rihanna*
Lady Gaga	*Kate Winslet*	*Victoria Beckham*
Justin Bieber	*Kristen Stewart*	*Brittany Snow*
Tom Cruise	*Winona Ryder*	*Jessica Simpson*
Charlize Theron	*Boy George*	*Taylor Swift*
Rob Pattinson	*Zac Efron*	*Justin Timberlake*
Taylor Launter	*Tom Felton*	*Kate Middleton*
Christian Bale	*Jason Segel*	*Julian Clary*
Barack Obama	*Jessica Alba*	*Daniel Radcliff*
Christine Aguilera	*Jackie Chan*	*Mika*
Katie Perry	*Michelle Trachtenburg*	*Eminem*
Madonna	*Chris Colfer*	*Jennifer Lawrence*
Ellen DeGeneres	*Rosario Dawson*	*Paul Potts*
Charlotte Dawson	*Megan Fox*	*Christina Hendricks*
Emma Watson	*Chad Michael Murray*	

The thread that ties these people together is a shared experience of bullying, abuse and intimidation in one form or another. All the people listed have achieved varying degrees of success or acclaim. Some continued to lead full and productive lives and overcome the derision and hurt that bullying inflicted, some struggled with the pressure.

As this is by no means a comprehensive list and given that many, many others have stories of abuse, intimidation and persecution, my question is: does bullying inevitably bring you down? Or could it potentially create an opportunity whereby the opinion of others becomes less of a driver? Could the experience of being bullied cause you to dig deep? Is it possible that bullying and intimidation can push you towards your purpose in life and help liberate you from the toxic effects of people-pleasing?

Evidently, to avoid being exposed to bullying in some form is nigh on impossible. It seems that being confronted with ridicule, condemnation and derision is a fairly inevitable experience for those who choose to reach for their dreams and follow the road less travelled. If you are feeling isolated, unwanted, rejected or unworthy simply because you are being bullied, it might be time to recognise that you in fact belong to the vast majority, as this is a worldwide, endemic and widespread phenomenon. There is no aloneness in this problem. The question isn't so much who is being bullied and why, the question is how do they handle it and more importantly, how are you going to handle it?

Successful strategies to overcome bullying include accepting that at times you may find yourself under fire and will need to take it as an opportunity to learn and use it to create a better experience for yourself in the future. It is highly probable that you will initially take the abuse personally, especially if it is particularly cruel or hostile. Instead of remaining stuck in the problem and focusing on

"It gets better. It seems hard, you know, I think being different is always going to be a tough climb. There's always going to be people that are scared of it. But at the end of the day you give those bullies, those people, that are so ignorant, if you give them the power to affect you, you're letting them win. And they don't deserve that. What you're doing by being yourself is you're keeping it real, and you're being really brave"

Adam Lambert

the words and actions of bullies, a healthier choice would be to turn your attention to the people and places that do support you, and the opportunities for creativity, plans, dreams and goals.

The world provides us with all kinds of experiences, and a great measure of success or failure depends on our willingness and ability to respond effectively to challenges that face us. It is not what happens to us that defines us, it is how we respond.

Perhaps, like the processes of giving birth, running a marathon, passing important exams, learning a new skill or in fact any great achievement in life, bullying gives you an opportunity to face and overcome the challenge of not being supported, not being loved and not being understood. Akin to a rite of passage, perhaps this very experience helps you to discover your own sense of self and move beyond the desire to please others. Is bullying potentially a great gift that pushes you to step away from limiting patterns and follow your own heart? Is it possible that bullying itself is paradoxically the catalyst for personal growth and development? Does learning how to overcome and manage bullying actually make you stronger?

"Always forgive your enemies— nothing annoys them so much"

Oscar Wilde

Physical bullying, however, has no place in this discussion and requires a zero tolerance approach. If you find yourself being physically intimidated in any shape or form then my unequivocal advice is to move yourself out of that situation and out of harm's way as soon as you can. A child at school requires the intervention and support of the school authorities, an employee requires the intervention and support of the management and a spouse or child in the home requires the intervention and support of the relevant authorities and support agencies in their area.

If these systems are unable to intervene effectively then the onus is on you to move away from the situation as soon as you can and find the right person or organisation to talk to. There is help out there for you, keep looking.

Why do bullies bully? *Because they can.* You may not have control over whether or not a bully shows up in your life and you may never truly understand why they chose to bully you, but you certainly do have control over how you feel and what you do about it.

To receive negative, unwanted, aggressive, derisory, unpleasant, or hurtful attention, is *not* an indication of your value or worth. Perhaps this very attention is more an indication of your untapped potential and the seeds of greatness that lie within you. Perhaps this unwanted attention indicates you have the potential to differentiate and step into your own power. Perhaps the bullying will give you space and time to figure out who you are and what you really want. Perhaps the bullying is a gift.

"The difference between feeling bullied and feeling empowered is self belief. You cannot be made to feel small,
you can only choose to feel so"

Out of the Depths - *Ed's Story*

"Happiness depends upon ourselves"

Aristotle

After years marching in high school bands, competing in the Jr. Drum Corps, touring with the USAF World Wide Talent Contests and performing in local bands, Ed Francis decided to bring his passion for percussion into the heart of his community. He began teaching as a drum coach at Round Rock Drums and also co-founded Rhythm Workshops, a non-profit organisation which works with special needs and disadvantaged communities to bring the magic of drumming to kids who would otherwise have little access to making music.

Ed never forgot how music and drumming helped him cope with the pain of growing up in an abusive and dysfunctional home environment. The scars may have run deep, but the power of a positive outlet helped to build his self-confidence and slowly release the debilitating anxieties building up in the young man.

Ed contributed this story to illustrate the stark and painful reality many children face and why it is so important to reach out in a meaningful way to these children when they are at school. He is a shining beacon of hope for those who do not believe in themselves.

Next time you see a greasy-haired, miserable kid at school, go over and say hello. It might be the next Ed Francis in the making and he could really do with a friend.

"I would not write these words if it wasn't for my firm belief that telling my story might help other people who have been through, are going through, or will go through similar experiences. I hope you are encouraged, and come to know that you are not alone.

My brother and I lived with our mother and stepfather. I do not wish to share too much about the conditions of our home but suffice to say that from nine until 15 years old, my life was painful and challenging.

One night my brother snuck into my room. He was mad at me and demanded, "You're the big brother, why don't you do something?" I wanted to do something, anything, but I was a frightened kid and had no idea what could be done. The guilt of not being able to help my little brother hurt. I felt helpless and ashamed as I watched my brother cry. All I could do was suffer in silence.

During the day one of my biggest challenges was to not be noticed. I receded deep within myself to where I felt I could almost disappear from the rest of the world. I remember moving very quietly around the house, especially while walking down the betraying wooden stairs which creaked loudly. Freeing myself from the confines of my house was an accomplishment, though the world outside my private hell was also full of its own obstacles and dangers.

I found myself to be different than most other children at school. I preferred to be by myself and many of my classmates had difficulty relating to this strange kid. My artistic side further separated me from others as I enjoyed drawing—something not requiring interactions with others. I was greasy, awkward and my social skills were lacking.

There are so many stories of what I endured. What I remember the most are the locations; waiting for the school bus in the mornings, on the school bus, in the classroom before the teacher arrived, the hallways between classes, walks home from school, sitting in my chair before Sunday School started, and perhaps worst of all—in my own house.

I felt alone, uncared for, and as if a huge target was painted on my shirt inviting others to take a shot at me. The kids who bullied me were many and they were not confined to the boys. Even some girls took it upon themselves to push me around and call me names. I was lost and didn't have the ability to stand up for myself, and others somehow knew it.

I remember asking myself, 'What did I do to deserve being treated this way? Why won't they just leave me alone? What's wrong with me that I draw so much attention to myself? Is there a place where I can break away from all this pain?'

Life didn't seem fair. Home wasn't a safe place and the rest of the world wasn't helping. No one appeared to care and I felt a need to transport myself to...anywhere. Anywhere but where I was at.

Escape found me in the form of a man who opened his home to some of us teenage boys. There I tasted freedom, and could relax. He bought us snacks, rented cool movies and we all had fun. Over time things changed, and he introduced us to pornography, X-rated videos, cigars and alcohol. He would even expose himself and touch us inappropriately. Where I thought I had found a friend I had instead found a hebephile.

It was at this point that I began marching in a junior drum and bugle corps, the Toreadors. We took pride in what we were doing and I started making real friends. A sense of purpose welled in my heart, and for the very first time I didn't feel lost—I was figuring out who I was and what I was capable of doing. It felt great to be good at something and have other kids recognise my burgeoning talents.

Music and drumming became my safe place. The group rehearsals and marching competitions were held far away from the chaos of my house, and hitting the drums grew into a constructive and much needed outlet for my growing anxieties. Things really started getting better. Instead of worrying about the disorder in my house, and what other kids were going to do to me, I was focusing on where I wanted to go and looking forward to my time doing shows with my friends in the Toreadors. I was happy.

Even with all the positive changes happening I still had to deal with the reality of what was happening in my house. Although I was going through a metamorphosis, the atmosphere at home continued to deteriorate.

One day I had had enough. I was 15 years old when my stepfather declared that I was no longer allowed to play the drums or take part in the drum and bugle corps. I was furious at the idea of losing the best part of my life. Something new clicked inside me. A part that had been missing, a sense of self-confidence, suddenly emerged.

We were standing at the top of the staircase, and as my stepfather continued yelling and spitting at me I decided to stand up for myself. I was scared, shaking uncontrollably, and my stomach was in knots as I looked up at the enraged man who had been the source of so much pain. I somehow managed to tell him that he wasn't going to take my drums away. I would no longer be living in his house, and didn't want him as my dad any more.

I remember rushing down the stairs hoping my stepfather would not follow, and ran as quickly as I could to my grandparents' home.

I got away!

I also 'got a way' to start living and begin taking ownership over what was happening in my life.

As I look back at everything that transpired during my youth, several things stand out:

- ❀ *It wasn't my fault*
- ❀ *The people who failed me and bullied me had their own issues*
- ❀ *I could choose to forgive others for my own benefit*
- ❀ *There's always a way out.*

So—what has been happening in my life since I got away?

I am now the drum coach and owner at Round Rock Drums, and co-founder (alongside my talented wife, Kim Francis) of our non-profit Rhythm Workshops. We also have five teenage boys, and remain actively involved in our community.

My work has allowed me to discover my life's mission: to help young people discover how truly special they are. I travel and speak to kids at schools, libraries, juvenile detention facilities, and anywhere groups of children can hear my message of being able to follow their dreams. These kids watch our student drummers perform and have an opportunity to actively participate in all the percussive fun. Our students have been featured on talk shows and play a leadership role in the lives of other kids by teaching the benefits of music and drumming.

My story is not unique. Many have been through misery and survived, even thrived. There are still young people living in similar circumstances right now; maybe you, or someone you know. Still more will experience the same horrible things in their future.

The best part about all the crap that happens is that we can choose to no longer stay stuck living in that part of our lives.

We can move on.

No matter what our history is, no matter how hurt we may have been, we are the authors of our own happiness and we can all have a positive impact on the rest of the world. Yes, even you!

What's your story?

How would you write the next chapter of your life?

Ed Francis
Founder/Drum Coach—Round Rock Drums
CEO/Co-Founder—Rhythm Workshops
www.roundrockdrums.com
www.rhythmworkshops.org

Five Myths of Bullying

"Nothing splendid has ever been achieved except by those who dared believe that something inside them was superior to circumstance"

Bruce Barton

One of the biggest obstacles we have in addressing the problem of bullying is the stigma and shame that surround the subject. This is largely created by a lack of understanding which in itself has created myths and misconceptions that serve to perpetuate the problem. Five of the most common myths around bullying are:

1. MYTH – Bullies are strong people

Truth – The desire to dominate another is a demonstration of weakness. People who feel the need to dominate another person will be, at some level, experiencing a sense of lack or fear within themselves. A person who is centred, balanced and in their own power has no need to bully. Although some bullies may well be physically strong and/or have a quick mind which allows them to dominate using intimidation, they experience themselves as 'less than' and use bullying as a means of increasing their sense of self-worth by overpowering or overwhelming another. This is generally a smokescreen used to bluff the world into seeing them as strong.

Some bullies are not physically strong or adept. Many are not particularly good fighters or able to physically dominate at all. Bullies by definition are insecure and uncertain of their own abilities and therefore attempt to create the *illusion* of strength. Their ability lies in being able to psychologically dominate and give the *impression* of having the upper hand. This kind of dominant behaviour is not strong, not powerful, not wise and more importantly not kind. Bullies are skilled at finding other people's pain point and applying pressure, they are not skilful at being strong.

The need to bully demonstrates a lack of self-control and a lack of understanding of true personal power. Bullies are out of alignment with themselves and are looking for external validation and/or reaction as at a deeper level have lost sight of themselves. Bullying is, on the whole, a demonstration of fear, insecurity and lack of confidence. This is not strength.

2. MYTH – Bullies seek out weak people

Truth – The irony is that bullies are often attracted to people who possess the very qualities they secretly or unknowingly admire. These qualities can often include emerging leadership, musical or artistic qualities, kindness, compassion, gentleness, creativity, quirkiness, out-of-the-box or independent thinking, inspiration and love. Many of these qualities will be portrayed by the bully and their entourage as weaknesses.

Just as pack animals attempt to divide and conquer when in search of prey, so bullies will see 'difference' as being a weakness and seek out people who appear to be different or who belong to minority groups. They use the advantage of numbers and community to dominate and control others. At times like these you will need to dig deep into your sense of self and self-worth and bide your time until you are able find yourself in a more supportive environment.

3. MYTH – Bullying is a schoolyard problem

Truth – Although schoolyard bullying is common, there are many other places in our society where dominating behaviours manifest. Some parents use intimidation or aggression towards their own children and each other, children can intimidate their siblings and/or parents, teachers bully students, students bully teachers and each other, sports coaches bully protégés, sports parents bully and intimidate from the sidelines, sports professionals use intimidation as a competitive tactic, managers intimidate staff, staff intimidate managers and their peers, corporations bully governments and vice versa, governments bully each other, and countries go to war.

Bullying is an 'equal opportunities experience' and can strike any person, in any place, at any time.

4. MYTH – Being bullied is shameful

Truth – There is no shame in being the target of bullying, in fact it can generally be taken as a somewhat perversely skewed compliment. Many genuinely awe-inspiring people have been bullied throughout history. The truth is, it is highly likely that every one of us will at some time or another come into contact with a bully. A great question to ask yourself at that time could be 'How can I remain optimistic, inspired and in my personal power?' along with 'How can I get out of this mess as quickly as possible?'

5. MYTH – Bullies are bad people

Truth – More often than not, bullies have either experienced significant bullying in their own lives, are deeply insecure or carry some internal and generally unconscious and unexpressed pain. Bullies are victims who are lashing out. Victims are bullies who bully themselves. Whilst we cannot condone or support the actions of bullies, perhaps we could see things through a broader perspective and inject some compassion into the mix.

"Compassion and happiness are not a sign of weakness but a sign of strength"

Dalai Lama

Facts and Figures

"There are three kinds of lies:
lies, damned lies, and statistics"

Benjamin Disraeli

The National Inquiry into the Impact of Violence on Young Australians (2009) found that the overwhelming majority of children and young people are not involved in violence either as victims or perpetrators.

Bullying is a problem; there is no doubt about that. What is in question is whether it is increasing or not. School and workplace reporting, along with media and social media exposure have propelled bullying into the public eye but this does not denote an increase. Bullying, intimidation and human rights abuses have been apparent in society since the dawn of time, just ask the cavemen.

There were many documented cases of school bullying and abuses of children in the 1800s, particularly during the Industrial Revolution (which is incidentally, when our current hierarchical education system was formed).

Historically, human beings have been a comparatively hostile and harsh species, preferring dominance and control tactics over negotiation and conciliation. While human beings appear on the surface to be inclined to use force to assert themselves, there are also many people who do not believe this to be the way forward. Conflict arises when these two opposing philosophies clash.

What has changed the face of bullying in our workplace and schools is increased awareness, as well as the introduction of formal anti-bullying programmes. This has caused a shift of consciousness and increased sensitivity to the problem. Another significant change is the rising prevalence of cyber bullying, which is a result of rapidly evolving technology, mobile phone use and social media.

Covert and cyber bullying differ from overt bullying in that many more people can be involved. There is a strong need for schools and workplaces to have a prompt and clear procedure when bullying has been identified, as it is insidious by nature and can have far-reaching consequences.

Measuring the problem of covert and cyber bullying with some degree of accuracy is rather difficult particularly as it does go largely unreported. We will, however, look at some of the more observable characteristics of bullying and the impact it is having on our children and youth.

To give the problem some context here is some interesting data from the Australian Covert Bullying Prevalence Study conducted by Edith Cowan University in 2009:

❀ Approximately one in four Year 4 to Year 9 Australian students (27%) report being bullied every few weeks

❀ Frequent school bullying was highest among Year 5 and Year 8 students

❀ 83% of students who bully others online, also bully others offline

❀ 84% of students who were bullied online were also bullied offline

❀ Hurtful teasing was the most prevalent of all bullying behaviours experienced by students, followed by having hurtful lies told about them.

"We should meet abuse by forbearance.
Human nature is so constituted that if we take absolutely no notice of anger or abuse, the person indulging in it will soon weary of it and stop"

Mahatma Gandhi

Given that bullying carries with it a stigma of shame, coupled with fear of retribution, much of the bullying that occurs will never be reported. For that reason we are focusing on strategies and solutions to overcome bullying as opposed to bullying per se.

According to the Australian Human Rights Commission the following fall under the umbrella of unacceptable human rights abuses:

All types of violence, harassment and bullying are harmful and unacceptable. The Committee on the rights of the child has clearly stated that there are no exceptions to this. To emphasise this the UN Committee on the Rights of the Child defines violence as including all forms of physical and mental violence including forms of violence that may be legal.

In Australia children and young people experience violence, harassment and bullying in a wide range of contexts and places these include:

Corporal (or physical) punishment is any type of punishment that uses physical force and is intended to cause pain or discomfort, however light. It includes hitting ("smacking", "slapping", "spanking"), with the hand or other implement, kicking, shaking or

throwing, scratching, pinching, biting, pulling hair or ears, forcing children to stay in uncomfortable positions, burning, scalding or forced ingestion (e.g. washing children's mouths out with soap). Some physical punishment of children is legal making its extent difficult to measure.

Source: bullying.humanrights.gov.au

It may come as a surprise to some parents that along with bullying, corporal punishment of children including washing children's mouths out with soap is considered an abuse of power. Ultimately and thankfully, it is now widely accepted that corporal punishment impacts negatively on a child's confidence and self-esteem and is not in the best interests of parent or child.

"He who commits injustice is ever made more wretched than he who suffers it"

Plato

Signs and Symptoms of Bullying

"I freed a thousand slaves. I could have freed a thousand more if only they knew they were slaves"

Harriet Tubman

Many parents are concerned that their child might be a victim of bullying. Some of the signs that a child is being bullied include:

- Increasing signs of depression, anxiety or stress
- Faltering self-esteem and self-image
- Reluctance or refusal to go to school
- Decline in school performance
- Unusually hungry after school
- Unexplained bruises, scrapes or injuries
- Unwillingness to discuss school
- Pattern of withdrawal, shame, fearfulness and anger
- Becomes stressed or withdrawn after using the computer or phone
- Persistent, vague, unexplained physical complaints
- Refuses to catch the bus or take the usual route to school
- Damaged or missing belongings
- Diminished social contacts
- Trouble sleeping or eating
- Inexplicably needs more money for school.

Equally you should be on the alert for signs that your child is a bully. Child bullying behaviour should be treated as a red flag to parents or educators as it can be a precursor to difficulties later in life. Habitual bullying can also profoundly affect future professional and personal relationships. It is important that children learn to express themselves in socially acceptable ways, and importantly, to discover more life-enhancing and valuable behaviours. Here are some of the indicators that your child may be a bully:

- ❀ Views violence positively
- ❀ Frequently teases or taunts other children
- ❀ Does not recognise bullying as a problem
- ❀ Persists in certain inappropriate or unpleasant behaviour even after being told to stop
- ❀ Accepts violence as a solution to problems
- ❀ Has a poor relationship with parents
- ❀ Is overly concerned with being and staying popular
- ❀ Is interested in extremely aggressive video games
- ❀ Seems intolerant of, and shows contempt for, children who are different
- ❀ Witnesses parents excluding, dominating, gossiping about, or otherwise hurting others
- ❀ Shows little sympathy to others who are being bullied, or empathy for those who are having problems
- ❀ Is friends with children who are violent or who bully
- ❀ Has experienced violence or abuse in the home
- ❀ Has a need to dominate others or control situations
- ❀ Is easily frustrated or discouraged
- ❀ Is regularly in trouble at school
- ❀ Shows either verbal or physical aggression toward adults as well as other children
- ❀ Is exclusive—refuses to include certain kids in play or study
- ❀ Hurts animals or takes pleasure in witnessing suffering.

"Keep your thoughts positive because your thoughts become your words.
Keep your words positive because your words become your behaviours.
Keep your behaviours positive because your behaviours become your habits.
Keep your habits positive because your habits become your values.
Keep your values positive because your values become your destiny."

Mahatma Gandhi

Am I a Bully?

"At age 20, we worry about what others think of us. At 40, we don't care what they think of us. At 60, we discover they haven't been thinking of us at all"

Ann Landers

Becky was around 12 years old and had been friends with Felicity throughout primary school although they had little in common. Their friendship was more of a convenience than a conscious desire to share experiences. In high school, Becky made a new friend, Emily, who took the same bus and lived relatively close by. They began to see each other outside of school and as their friendship blossomed, Becky's friendship with Felicity suffered. Emily and Felicity didn't get along so Becky, finding school now rather awkward, decided to tell Felicity that she wanted to hang out with Emily instead of her during break times. This caused Felicity great distress and they never spoke again.

The question is, was Becky a bully?

In fact, Becky displays a normal if somewhat juvenile and insensitive approach to the phenomenon of growing apart. Although her behaviour could be perceived as mean or unkind, she was at least being honest. This is a normal experience and many relationships break down as a result of the same pattern. Becky was not bullying although her actions did hurt Felicity's feelings quite badly. Hurting someone's feelings or moving in different directions is not bullying, although it can feel harsh and unforgiving at the time.

In exploring if you are a bully, ask yourself if you use strength, position or influence to harm, intimidate or force on those who are more vulnerable or ill-equipped to adequately defend themselves. If you answer yes, you are a bully.

However, if you feel drawn to ask yourself these kinds of questions then there is a good chance that, as well-intentioned and as kind-hearted as you are, you may at times be perceived as a bully.

When an outwardly confident, high energy, action orientated individual meets a self-conscious, reserved and reflective person who dislikes attention and has difficulty speaking up or saying no, then the former may unbeknownst to them be perceived by the latter as a bully. The willingness and ability to speak up for yourself and be heard often plays a part in the confusion and miscommunication that exists between bully and victim.

As bullying is often concealed by both the bully and the victim, it is important to pay attention to what is going on with your children. Watch for signs that he or she is being bullied, or that he or she is a bully, and take action to help them. Both situations are an opportunity for growth and development. Bullying, when caught early on, can be easily diffused and serve as a great life lesson. Bullying is commonplace and in the early stages does not cause long-term damage. When left unchecked it can provoke more serious problems.

If you are concerned that your child may be a bully but do not know what to do, begin with your child's teacher, student well-being officer or paediatrician to figure out a plan. Bullies need to understand why they behave the way they do, and what they can change. Inevitably a child that is bullying is doing so because they are in pain or have some need that is not being met, and a child that is bullied is likely to be suffering. As a parent, responsible adult or caregiver it is your job to help them.

"Hatred can be overcome only by love"

Mahatma Gandhi

Why Bullies Attack

"Hear the other side"

St. Augustine

In the 1984 movie *Karate Kid* a young boy finds himself far from his own culture, feeling alone and unhappy. He experiences unbearable bullying and physical abuse from students at his new school before he discovers a wise mentor. The boy then learns karate, trains very hard to overcome his difficulties and ultimately finds peace and personal power within himself. He chooses to remain in his integrity and does not use his new skills to attack his aggressors. Instead, he enters a sporting competition to demonstrate to himself and the world that he has the power and potential to overcome abuse and intimidation.

This movie serves not only as a metaphor but also as a reminder that bullying is a global and cross-cultural problem.

Bullying is often honoured and glorified by the media and computer gaming industry. Given the content of an average Saturday night's television, it appears many of us are quite comfortable viewing acts of violence and crime. We don't tend to question the value of watching graphic images and movies, exposing our children to the horrors of war, sexual violence and crime every evening on the news, and yet find ourselves confused by the prevalence of bullying in schools.

If we were truly committed to eliminating bullying from our cultural story then we would be mindful of our willingness to expose both ourselves and our children to sensational negative media, movies, internet games and the imagery that accompanies it. We would be asking to what degree we accept aggression and violence within our day to day environment, and what do we classify as real and present danger.

Human beings, despite a fierce attachment to our independence and rights and our reliance on our intellect to steer us in the right direction, are easily manipulated. The advertising, marketing and political worlds depend on this. Our ability to readily take on information is part of our survival

> *"Mastering others is strength. Mastering yourself is true power"*
>
> Lao Tzu

mechanism. If we are receptive to our environment then we are able to adapt if necessary. This is all well and good if we were living in the wild and needed only to absorb and interpret our immediate environment in order to stay safe. It becomes more complicated when we are absorbing and interpreting information that has been cleverly constructed to catch our attention, fuel our fears and prejudices and leave us with a false sense of imminent danger.

Most of us don't enjoy being presented with a bully but in all probability we will meet them as we journey through life. A few years ago I listened to an audio by Dr. John Demartini where he discussed the premise that in life you can be assured that around 33% of people will like you, 33% of people will be indifferent to you and 33% of people will dislike you. That being so, the question is no longer whether you will be faced with people who challenge or oppose you, the more useful question to ask yourself is how do you deal with them.

> *"Physical strength can never permanently withstand the impact of spiritual force"*
>
> Franklin D. Roosevelt

To understand what provokes a bully to act, we need to first establish the back story. For a bully to feel compelled to action, they will have taken the information that surrounds them and determined that they are either threatened or inadequate in some way.

Bullying to a degree is a chest-beating exercise to establish the illusion of power and authority. This is often not directly incited by the person they are intimidating but that person is chosen in the anticipation that they are willing to give up ground fairly easily. The fact that a bully is prepared to use aggressively dominant behaviour shows they are feeling a sense of fear, lack or weakness which causes them to lash out.

The bully has two beliefs here, that (1) making someone else feel small will increase their sense of personal power and (2) they can actually *make* someone feel small. In fact bullying can only remind the victim that they have a sense of 'smallness' inside them that needs to be addressed.

The payoff for the bully's aggressive behaviour is at best a momentary distraction from their inner turmoil. Inevitably, as with all unresolved inner pain, the discomfort returns, and perhaps even increases, as a result of causing suffering to another person. Most are of course totally oblivious to this pattern as it is deeply embedded in the unconscious. The pattern is played out in the same way whether it be in schoolyards, marriages, relationships, politics or the business and corporate sectors.

Human beings are not innately aggressive or unkind. Unprovoked hostility is not our first instinct. We are more inclined to save, rescue and care for each other. There are countless heroic and inspiring stories about people who put themselves at risk to save complete strangers. This is testament to our evolution from a basic primal state and evidence of our intrinsically good essential nature. Babies will cry when they hear someone crying, toddlers will comfort each other, children and most adults will be easily distressed by anger or violence. Therefore, when faced with a bully, knowing that something has happened to them to distort the natural evolution of a healthy and happy individual, can at the very least, move you to a place of compassion.

"You have power over your mind – not outside events. Realise this, and you will find strength"

Marcus Aurelius

So, what can the victim do? In understanding the structure of bullying, the victim can very quickly notice that in fact they hold all the power.

⌘ They have a choice as to whether they behave aggressively or peacefully.

⌘ They have a choice as to whether they feel the need to take steps or not.

⌘ They have a choice as to whether they take the bully's behaviour to be an indication of their value and self-worth, or simply the expression of an individual who is in pain and seeking an avenue to channel through.

⌘ They have a choice as to whether they take the bully seriously and whether they stay in a situation where they are easily targeted.

You could argue that the bully also has a choice, and this would be true. However, bullies generally don't perceive the situation as a problem and are often not aware of or often even interested in the other choices that are available to them. The bully is not operating consciously, however the victim being in a more receptive space is better able to assess the situation and has many choices of how to react.

The victim is not a victim unless they choose to accept the role. The bully is driven by a need to dominate and overpower, which is in general outside their consciousness. They feel compelled to find a victim onto whom they can project their own suffering.

"If you want others to be happy, practice compassion. If you want to be happy, practice compassion"

Dalai Lama

If you refuse to play the game, the bully will continue searching until they find another. The whole bully/victim cycle requires that someone 'agrees' to be the victim. This cycle will only end when the bully tires of this pattern and seeks a different solution to their internal pain state.

If truth be known, generally the bullies themselves do not know why they bully and it's unlikely without a really compelling motivation they will attempt to understand what drives them to choose to be hurtful. It is important to remember that a bully sees you through the filter of their own personal view of life and as a reflection of themselves.

"You have enemies? Good. That means you've stood up for something, sometime in your life"

Winston Churchill

Uncomfortable Beginnings - *My Story*

"The things which hurt, instruct"

Benjamin Franklin

Now, in retrospect, I feel lucky and grateful that I was bullied in primary school. At the time it was deeply painful and upsetting and I didn't appreciate the essential confidence-building benefits the experience would ultimately bring me.

Back then, I couldn't figure out why I was targeted so regularly. I thought it might have been because I had too many brothers, or because I owned a pony (cardinal sin apparently), or perhaps because I was the only child at the Catholic school who did not regularly attend church (an actual sin). It felt to me that in the eyes of children, being different was a bad thing and to be avoided at all costs. I wished fervently that I could find a way to fit in and be accepted but there are some things that you just can't change.

This state of mind, combined with being quiet and shy made me very easy pickings. I was also extremely skinny, which I believed rendered me hideously ugly. My skinniness was acutely painful to me and the fact that it drew so much attention was almost more than I could bear. Ironically, the fact that I have remained fairly skinny is even now deeply irritating to many of my friends but for completely different reasons.

Bullies found me captivating and focused a great deal of unwelcome attention in my direction. In my school in the not-so-soft north of England, there was one girl in particular who decided I had superb victim potential. I will call her Nadine, although this is of course not her real name. Nadine didn't like me much at all. To make matters worse, she was about a foot taller than me, very athletic and muscle-bound, which was a tad intimidating.

One day, when I was about eight years old, I arrived at school to find that no one in my group of friends was talking to me. Not only were they not talking to me, they wouldn't even look at me. I was utterly rejected and outcast, which was extremely confusing and deeply hurtful, especially as the group included my good friend Maddie. Apparently Nadine had decided that I was 'out' of the group and forbade them from having any contact with me. This treatment lasted for around a week. A few days after my exclusion, Maddie secretly handed me a letter in which she apologised for not talking to me and swore her undying love and support. She wrote that she felt compelled to abide by Nadine's rules but wanted me to know that she loved me and felt terrible about the whole thing. Cold comfort really, to an eight-year-old outcast.

This problem continued in varying degrees throughout primary school. Eventually Nadine and I went to the same high school, but luckily we had very little contact with each other. That was until one evening at the local youth club during one of my very early, very self-conscious social experiences as a pre-teen. I have an awful feeling that I might have been wearing deep pink shiny satin trousers, which was all good until I arrived and realised everyone else was in jeans and sweatshirts.

> "The ultimate measure of a man is not where he stands in moments of comfort and convenience, but where he stands at times of challenge and controversy"
>
> Martin Luther King, Jr

Maddie, my not-so-loyal friend, was moving away and we were having a little farewell gathering to say goodbye. We were sitting together around a table and for some reason Maddie thought it would be funny to tap me with her shoe. Not being a huge fan of germs I wasn't terribly thrilled about having a dirty shoe tapped on my arm. Despite my protests she wouldn't stop. Eventually, I loudly and heatedly told her to leave me alone.

Unbeknownst to me, Nadine was watching us from a distance and came flying over. She towered over me like a giant raging inferno whilst I sat stunned in my chair, a skinny wisp of a 12-year-old trying to make sense of the nonsensical. She glared at me like an angry fire-breathing dragon and instructed me to step outside and *fight* her. It was so ridiculous, almost comical, like a Woody Allen movie script.

I think it was at that moment I snapped. I had had enough. I was so sick and tired of years of being intimidated and pushed around and for the first time outside the safety of my own home I became wild with anger. I stood up and yelled, as loudly as I could, "Are you out of your mind? Have you seen the size of you and the size of me? Has it not occurred to you that we are girls? If you think for one second that I am going to go out into a car park so that you can mash me into the ground then you have got another think coming!"

She was so shocked by my reaction, as were we all, that she deflated on the spot. Nadine turned and walked away and that was that.

A few weeks later she approached me on the school bus and for the first time in all the years of our relationship spoke honestly and openly. She apologised for her behaviour and explained that she was having problems at home. She was an adopted child with a difficult, dominant and aggressive father and things had not been going well for her. She was hurting badly that evening at the youth club and had lashed out at me. This lesson has served me well over time and still serves to remind me of the need for compassion, regardless of the unfairness or harshness of the circumstances we find ourselves in.

In truth, who was the victim in my childhood life story, and who won that battle? Who experienced suffering during those years and who in fact needed help? If your answer was the both of us, you are absolutely right.

"The best way out is always through"

Robert Frost

Why Me?

"My philosophy is: It's none of my business what people say of me and think of me. I am what I am and I do what I do. I expect nothing and accept everything. And it makes life so much easier"

Anthony Hopkins

If you have been the subject of a bully's attentions, you will have undoubtedly asked yourself the age old question 'Why me?' Curiously, this turns out to be the worst question you could possibly ask, as it generally results in a drawn-out, disheartening, intellectual struggle to make sense out of the nonsensical. In relation to solving the bullying problem, *NEVER, EVER* ask yourself 'why are they bullying me?' or worse, 'what is wrong with me, or why don't they like me?'

Unless you are in a close relationship with the bully, such as a married couple, and intend to challenge the status quo in order to improve the relationship, these questions will lead you on a pointless and fruitless quest. This is particularly the case for schoolchildren. The schoolyard is not a place to resolve long-standing, deep-seated psychological, personal or behavioural issues. It does not serve a child to look so deeply into the problem.

Instead, ask yourself why you are so keen to understand the thinking of someone whose opinion in all probability, you do not respect or agree with. Rather, focus on what you need to do to turn this situation around.

"Life is not the way it's supposed to be. It's the way it is. The way you cope with it is what makes the difference"

Virginia Satir

One child I spoke with was worried about being unpopular in class, and having a tough time being teased and put down by some of the other students. I asked her what special talents she had, what gifts she possessed and what kind of a woman she would grow into. She told me that she didn't know. "Ah ha," I said, "Given that even you don't know what specialness lies inside you yet, how can the kids in your class possibly know that you have no worth and no value?"

If we have not yet discovered our true potential or personal power, why would we allow someone outside of ourselves to define or decide our worth? Just as a seed spends a great deal of time buried under the soil before it germinates, so human potential lies largely hidden from view until it is ready. Not being able to see it doesn't mean it isn't there. Sometimes believing really is seeing. If no one else can see or establish your true worth, then your belief and self-confidence are the only true gauge of who you really are and what you are capable of.

If a person is bullying you, they are displaying behaviour which does not merit respect or support. A bully will not be able or indeed willing to acknowledge your potential, value and worth and is far more likely to wish to diminish or inhibit you; you would be better served not waiting for their approval. Instead, focus on what needs to be done so that you can place your energy and attention elsewhere.

"It is our enemies that provide us with the challenge we need to develop the qualities of tolerance, patience and compassion"

Dalai Lama

Perception and Projection

"Projections change the world into the replica of one's own unknown face"

Carl Jung

Projection is a theory espoused by Swiss psychiatrist and psychotherapist Carl Jung as an unconscious process where we see aspects of ourselves in others. We defend ourselves against our distasteful impulses by denying their existence, while attributing them to others. For example, a person who is deceitful may be prone to accusing other people of deceit.

Projection occurs when a person responds negatively to perceived deficiencies in another, due to unresolved conflict at the unconscious level. In short, we blame the other for aspects of ourselves we choose not to recognise or acknowledge.

Whenever a person is emotionally charged and *resistant to* negative aspects of another person, a projection is mostly likely being engaged. This does not mean that these qualities are absent in the other person. It merely means that there is unresolved conflict in the person observing them. As this is an unconscious process it requires a great deal of self-awareness to overcome.

The NLP Communication Model asserts that we create our projections, based on the filters we use to interpret the world around us. These filters are influenced by our life experiences and more importantly our *perception* of these experiences. When we look at a tree, we access our memory filter to bring up our previous experience of trees; our language filter to describe the tree; our values, beliefs and attitude filters to decide what a tree means to us, and our decision filter to form our conclusion about the tree. There are other filters we run at the same time and each filter is personal and specific to us. Just as no two people have the same fingerprint, no two people have the same filters.

The perceptions we have are entirely dependent on our previous

"Everything that irritates us about others can lead us to an understanding of ourselves"

Carl Jung

experience, memories and the interpretation and conclusions we have drawn. Our perception colours every experience that we have and is the reason why human beings find it so very difficult to communicate the concept of a universal truth and reality.

Perception is the methodology or means by which we form conclusions about life, and projection is the *meaning* we ascribe to the people, places and things in our environment as a result of our perceptions.

For instance, two people walking through a park in the sunshine are able to have completely contradictory experiences. One may feel calm, serene and connected to the beauty that surrounds them. The other may feel threatened and exposed, fearful of wildlife or potential threats. The external circumstances are the same but each person applies different filters (perceptions) and comes to different conclusions (projections).

> *It was six men of Indostan*
> *To learning much inclined,*
> *Who went to see the Elephant*
> *(Though all of them were blind),*
> *That each by observation*
> *Might satisfy his mind.*
>
> *The First approach'd the Elephant,*
> *And happening to fall*
> *Against his broad and sturdy side,*
> *At once began to bawl:*
> *"God bless me! but the Elephant*
> *Is very like a wall!"*
>
> *The Second, feeling of the tusk,*
> *Cried, "Ho! what have we here*
> *So very round and smooth and sharp?*
> *To me 'tis mighty clear*
> *This wonder of an Elephant*
> *Is very like a spear!"*
>
> *The Third approached the animal,*
> *And happening to take*
> *The squirming trunk within his hands,*
> *Thus boldly up and spake:*
> *"I see," quoth he, "the Elephant*

Is very like a snake!"
The Fourth reached out his eager hand,
And felt about the knee.
"What most this wondrous beast is like
Is mighty plain," quoth he,
"'Tis clear enough the Elephant
Is very like a tree!"

The Fifth, who chanced to touch the ear,
Said: "E'en the blindest man
Can tell what this resembles most;
Deny the fact who can,
This marvel of an Elephant
Is very like a fan!"

The Sixth no sooner had begun
About the beast to grope,
Then, seizing on the swinging tail
That fell within his scope,
"I see," quoth he, "the Elephant
Is very like a rope!"

And so these men of Indostan
Disputed loud and long,
Each in his own opinion
Exceeding stiff and strong,
Though each was partly in the right,
And all were in the wrong!

MORAL

So oft in theologic wars,
The disputants, I ween,
Rail on in utter ignorance
Of what each other mean,
And prate about an Elephant
Not one of them has seen!

John Godfrey Saxe
Derived from Indian legend

If this is indeed true, it then follows that there is no single solution and no definitive reality, there is only what we believe we are seeing and experiencing. If your filters (values, beliefs, memories, decisions, attitudes) are set to 'I can't trust anybody', 'life is unfair', 'I never get what I want', 'all people lie', 'kind people are wimps', 'I have to fight to get my own way' or something equally debilitating, then you will experience that as your truth. If you are in a relationship with someone who has those filters operating you could easily find yourself being perceived as a threat or at the very least, a significant part of the problem.

This communication problem can cause difficulties when we project our 'stuff' onto others. Our reality is a creation that depends on previous life experience and is not necessarily the truth from a broader perspective.

A child who comes from a family with unstable parents may well, as an adult, project their fear and insecurities onto their life partner. They may see similarities and reflections that don't have any correlation to their current relationship. Fear of abandonment, fear of loss, fear of retribution and punishment can all cloud a perfectly healthy union and make things difficult for both parties. Equally, a child who has grown up in an abusive home may be inclined, as an adult, to overreact and use unreasonable behaviour or violence to resolve differences.

We are drawn to people who experience a similar reality to us but it is impossible to find someone who sees everything the way we do or who comes to all the same conclusions. Throughout our lifetime we will inevitably come across people who will challenge our version of reality. Just as we need to prune our plants to make way for new growth, being challenged about our decisions and beliefs gives us an opportunity to consider whether our path, choices, behaviours and conclusions are accurate or not. Challenge is good, it keeps us real.

"The best political, social, and spiritual work we can do is to withdraw the projection of our shadow onto others"

C.G. Jung

When you find yourself confronted with someone who appears to have got completely the wrong end of the stick about you, this merry dance and healthy interchange can turn rather nasty. Their filters may not permit them to see you as you imagine yourself to be and as such there is absolutely no point trying to persuade them otherwise. Ultimately, if a friend, acquaintance or family member consistently views you negatively, contradicts your idea of yourself, misjudges your intentions and motivations, and paints a very different picture of you to others, there is generally very little you can do to change their perception.

Regardless of the back story, life can and often does work out well for people who take responsibility for their behaviour. They understand that life is not black and white, attempt to see other people's perspectives and seek out growth and development opportunities. Problems occur for those who see the world as responsible for their experience and seek to attribute blame to others. Life is a constant struggle for people who refuse to take control of themselves and

"Reality doesn't bite, rather our perception of reality bites"

Anthony J. D'Angelo

their direction in life and who prefer to attribute blame to people, governments, environmental factors or even genetic and/or inherited traits.

Understanding the concept of projection allows you to appreciate why and how some people see you in such negative and unreasonable light and why they blame you for the emotions they are experiencing. It also accounts for why they are able to hold a picture of you that, in your opinion, is completely off the mark. Their projection clouds their understanding of who you really are and colours what they see.

Just as an optimistic person lives in fundamentally bright world, an angry person lives in an angry and hostile world. Ironically, people who look at the world predominantly through negative or critical eyes are attracted to those who look at the world through rose-coloured glasses. Interestingly, the traits of optimism and enthusiasm that attracted them can eventually become frustrating to a predominantly pessimistic or 'glass half empty' personality and this is when conflict can arise.

If you are around a person who is deeply invested in negative thinking, they will see faults and flaws in many things and many people around them, including you, *regardless of your behaviour*. The danger here is that if you are not vigilant or conscious enough of this you may well begin to see yourself through their eyes. You can inadvertently take on the role they have projected onto you, and by doing so you will confirm their opinion of the world. The cycle is then complete and a co-dependent relationship is formed which is of no benefit to either party in the long term.

If you find yourself in this situation and feel that someone is projecting their 'stuff' onto you, remind yourself that it is their challenge, not yours. Years ago, Wayne and I were having a furious argument over something inconsequential and he was giving me a long list of reasons why he felt so upset and why I was responsible for those feelings. I asked if he was implying that if he were not married to me the feelings of sadness, unhappiness, frustration would not occur. To his credit, he immediately realised what he was doing, stepped back into his personal power and took responsibility for his own emotions.

If you choose to remain stuck in a pattern of blaming others, not only will you find your relationship to be unfulfilling and unsatisfactory but you also relinquish any opportunities for growth and evolution.

"Fall seven times, stand up eight"

Japanese proverb

The Blame Game

"Blaming everyone and everything else for our problems and challenges may be the norm and may provide temporary relief from the pain, but it also chains us to these very problems. Show me someone who is humble enough to accept and take responsibility for his or her circumstances and courageous enough to take whatever initiative is necessary to creatively work his or her way through or around these challenges, and I'll show you the supreme power of choice"

The 7 Habits of Highly Effective People—
Steve Covey

Looking at successful people who have built lives which reflect their personal dreams and aspirations, it is clear that they do not give responsibility for their happiness to another, nor do they make excuses for their mistakes. On the contrary, they take full responsibility for their life experience, and do not expect happiness or success to be handed to them by another. They understand that these things emerge out of their consistent actions and choices. Errors are celebrated as developmental milestones or opportunities, as successful people are aware that making mistakes is a prerequisite to learning and growth. If you wish to expand your creative ability, you have to be willing to not only make plenty of mistakes, but to use every single one of them as a valued lesson.

Blame is a fool's game. Never take the blame for someone else's aggression or emotional state, nor blame them for the impact they are having on your life. Unless you are physically chained to an immovable object and have no physical freedom, then there are choices available to you and therefore you need to take responsibility for what is happening. If you are in pain and suffering, it is time to rethink your options and create a new strategy. Blaming the perpetrator is of no use to you, brings no relief and does not help you to solve your problem.

Just as it does not serve you to blame someone else for your situation, it equally does not serve you to blame yourself. Deciding that you are defective or should make adjustments to suit the demands of another is self-deprecating and pointless. If you are experiencing abuse it is immensely painful and time-consuming to focus on why the bullying is happening. It is extremely difficult to interpret what is going on in a bully's mind and regardless, we are never truly in a position to manage and control the emotional state of another.

"Whatever happens, take responsibility"

Tony Robbins

Inevitably, when a relationship or experience causes deep and enduring emotional pain or suffering, there will be an opportunity for growth. You will find these opportunities by addressing the aspect of yourself that is willing to feel victimised or belittled. If not, you will continue to experience and create the same challenging situation in future relationships. It would be beneficial to look at why and how you are creating a situation in which someone feels comfortable treating you badly. You can then work to lift your self-belief and self-confidence back to a healthy, relationship-sustaining level.

"Beliefs have the power to create and the power to destroy. Human beings have the awesome ability to take any experience of their lives and create a meaning that dis-empowers them or one that can literally save their lives"

Tony Robbins

Regardless of what other people think, we are all unique, valuable, and deserving of love and respect. Self-mastery comes about when we shift our focus from external circumstances to our internal condition. If we are waiting to feel loved, valued and respected through our relationships with another or through acclaim or achievement, we will be waiting a very long time. If we achieve external success and acclaim and fail to address how we see ourselves, we will continue to feel unloved, undervalued, disrespected or whichever negative perception we hold.

You possess the power to have a profound impact on this world. If you do not as yet recognise your gifts and potential, time and focused action is all that is required for them to come to life. Do not hand over responsibility for your happiness or your future to another and do not attribute blame for your circumstances to another. All the challenges and difficulties you have faced have delivered learning and understanding that *enhance* your life experience and help you become a better person.

As we have seen played out in our society countless times, no matter how many achievements you have, if you have not made peace with yourself, you will remain unhappy. If you address the relationship you have with yourself and discover how to feel loved, valued and deserving of respect *regardless* of your external circumstances, you will no longer seek external approval and will be well on the way to leading a happy and fulfilled life.

When a storm hits a town and knocks down the houses, you are not best served by asking yourself *why* the storm happened or *why* your house in particular was damaged. The pain that comes from those questions offers no closure or resolution. Healing begins when you ask yourself 'What shall I do about it? How do I proceed from here and what resources and tools do I have to improve or change the situation?' Healing begins when you make plans to turn tragedy into triumph. Growth occurs when you stop focusing on the problem and turn your energy and attention to the solution.

"If it's never our fault, we can't take responsibility for it. If we can't take responsibility for it, we'll always be its victim"

Richard Bach

Critical Acclaim - *Michael's Story*

"Beyond ideas of wrongdoing and right-doing, there is a field.
I'll meet you there"

Rumi

Michael Schwandt is one of the most dynamic contributors to choreography and movement in Los Angeles. His extensive body of work can be seen across the board in television, commercials, corporate industrials, music videos and live special events, crossing all genres of dance as both a stage director and choreographer.

Michael's credits include projects with Lady Gaga, Katy Perry, Kelly Rowland, David Guetta, John Legend, Flo Rida, Havana Brown, The Veronicas, Cirque du Soleil, Miss Universe, So You Think You Can Dance, America's Next Top Model, Ringling Bros, Michelle Obama, Nike for the World Cup and Olympics.

Michael's story strikes at the heart of the *From Bullied to Brilliant* message of personal power, self-belief, determination, perseverance and ultimately, success. Carving out a successful career in dance wasn't easy for a creative and artistic boy growing up in Texas in the 1990s. His willingness to share this important story can inspire those who dream a bigger dream to close their ears to the naysayers, breathe deep, lift their heads up, and reach for the stars. After all, it is clearly worth it.

"We moved a lot when I was a child, and I attended any given school for less than a year at a time. The social odds were against me as I generally found myself outside of established friendship groups. But all that moving gave me a thick skin and I learned how to cope with not fitting in. This was long before dance shows had made their way into the living rooms of people all over the world. Male dancers at that time were not considered socially acceptable, particularly by other men. I started dancing in my bedroom in Junior High in secret, trying to emulate Michael Jackson, Madonna and Janet Jackson. By the time we moved to Texas and I started

high school, I decided I was ready to go public with my unusual hobby.

My dance and choreography journey began with the high school talent show. I put together a dance troupe, we got in, and went on to win an award. This was the first time I had danced in front of other people, and the show I put together was a provocative performance for a high school talent show. That experience set the tone for me throughout high school.

I did theatre, ran track, played soccer and football and was an honour student, yet people only knew me as 'that weird guy who dances'. In Texas at that time football was everything. If you didn't play football or the like, you weren't respected as a man. There was a lot of animosity towards any guy who was willing to get on stage and dance in front of four or five hundred people. I decided to take this as a challenge and at every talent show I wanted to top what I'd done the year before.

I started getting positive attention from other students, then it spread to teachers and even parents. My burgeoning popularity created a lot of jealousy, but it took me a while to realise what was happening. I started hearing jokes, some talking behind my back. It was predominantly other guys, the ones who played sports. This was interesting because it was often their girlfriends who were cheering for me in the audience. It became so tough with my critics ostracising me that I stopped playing organised sports altogether. I didn't think I belonged.

No one was physically violent to me; it was more talking down to me, or swearing at me under their breath as they walked by. When I wore something different it was easy for people to call me a homo or a faggot. The general consensus was that because I was a guy who liked to dance, I must be gay, and this definitely wasn't socially acceptable. Regardless of whether I was or wasn't, it was a stigma created purely because of my choice to dance.

Of course it comes back to people being insecure and projecting that on to people who are different. The funny thing is, I had a lot of friends in school because I was successful at sports as well as academic studies. I was a competitive honour student. Still, my peers singled me out as the guy who didn't play football, who danced and choreographed performances.

It culminated during my senior year. At the beginning of the year I was voted homecoming king of my school, with my best friend coincidentally being homecoming queen. In Year Twelve, as a theatre student, I was to produce and direct my own show. This project would take a full year, and I chose, of all things, to put on 'The Girlie Show: Live Down Under' – a Madonna concert.

It was amazing. We had auditions for the show and over fifty students auditioned. There was strong competition for the lead, even the Madonna character. It was crazy! All the attention tipped things over for some people. A homecoming king who was putting on a production about Madonna, a gay icon, was just too much. The bullying came to a head, and even people I had thought were friends or had worked with on projects with stopped talking to me and inviting me to social gatherings that I would have previously been a part of.

I was well practiced at filtering out the abuse and not letting it bother me, but I still wanted to fit in, to be included. With the exception of a handful of friends, it became clear that this wasn't going to be the case for me. The bullying was worse in social settings where people were bolder with comments and more willing to make jokes or say things under their breath. As a consequence, going to parties or out with friends became difficult.

The bullying was never physical, but in some ways mental bullying and constant day-in and day-out comments were worse. It messes with you; it makes you question your self-worth, and yourself as a person. You wonder if you really are a freak, or if it really is bad to do something different from everyone else. It was tough going through this at my age, while I was discovering more about myself as a person and a man. It did get to me because I wanted acceptance. It bothered me that there were people out there who didn't like me. I thought it was ridiculous that people could dislike someone for what they liked to do with their spare time. I'm sure many of those people are eating their words now.

When I reflect today, I know that if I had given in to what people said, cared what people thought, listened to the criticism, or let name-calling or animosity affect me, I never would have got to where I am. You simply can't question yourself if you're aiming for success. There was always an innate ability inside me and a strong drive to not only succeed, but to exceed expectations. That's something I haven't lost to this day; I still apply it to every project I work on, no matter how large or small.

If you're going to be successful there can be no doing it halfway, and there can certainly be no doubting yourself or your ability. We all doubt ourselves at some time, but if I had doubted myself at that critical point in my life, I never would have gone on to do the things I've done. I never would have pushed myself, I never would have asked questions, and I never would have continued to succeed.

With modern social media interconnectivity, some of those people now send me friend requests or make comments on photos I post about projects I'm working on. These are people I haven't spoken to in fifteen years, since I was 'that weird guy who liked to dance'. Granted I had a lot of people who supported me, but you always remember the ones that don't.

It's so much easier for someone to tell you that you can't do something, to put you down, to criticise you and tell you that you are strange. It's so much easier and people love to do it, but those are the people you have to filter out so they don't dampen the flames of your success. I don't hate anyone for what they think about me, then or now. Without that contributing to my upbringing, my life experience and my journey, I never would have got to where I am now and I never would have achieved what I've achieved.

I'm still not done by any means – I still push myself as I know I haven't even seen the tip of the iceberg. There's so much more I want to do. To me what I've accomplished isn't enough, and I think that's a drive and a spirit that will never die. When I look back over what I've achieved in my twelve years working in this industry I know that many people won't accomplish half of those things in a lifetime, so I'm very thankful.

I'm thankful for everyone that ever told me I couldn't, everyone that wished me ill. I'm thankful for all my experiences and I'm very fortunate that my life was never in danger and my physical well-being was never threatened. I'm also happy that I had a strong enough personality to not let those experiences send me to a darker place. Because I know it's not the same for everyone – there are people out there who find it gets too much, who lack the confidence or self-belief to follow their dreams and for whom a mental beating up is enough to push them over into darkness, depression and despair.

For those people, I have to say that you must be strong, you must be true to who you are, and you must believe in yourself. Tomorrow is another day, next week is another week, and next year is another year. I can't tell you how many times I've had a bad experience and then looked back on that experience a year later, from such a different place in my life, and realised I've learnt so much and achieved so much and grown so much. You can't always focus on the moment – when bad things happen you have to have a positive outlook and look forward to the future. It's one of the only ways to keep your sanity, to find hope and know that this is just one small part of many, many, many parts of your life.

I sincerely hope that this book and its messages will reach people the world over. Hopefully what I have shared can also help somebody else turn adversity into achievement."

Michael Schwandt
Stage Director/Choreographer
www.michaelschwandt.com

Prejudice

"What luck for the rulers that men do not think"

Adolph Hitler

Oxford Dictionary:
   Prejudice: Preconceived opinion that is not based on reason or actual experience
   Racism: *The belief that all members of each race possess characteristics, abilities, or qualities specific to that race, especially so as to distinguish it as inferior or superior to another race or races.*

During my eight years in West Africa I had ample time to examine and consider the concepts of racism and prejudice and the connection they have with bullying and abuse. To me, the line between the two seemed somewhat blurry and ill-defined. Until that point in time, although well-versed in prejudice I had very little exposure to racism. Growing up in the north-west English countryside was an almost exclusively white Anglo-Saxon affair.

The Cote d'Ivoire couldn't have been more different. You might imagine that racism would be an overriding problem in such a culturally diverse area, but in the early 1980s it was a surprisingly peaceful place to live. The Cote d'Ivoire was a country that welcomed the arrival of expatriate workers along with the economic benefits they brought. There was a large Lebanese community running small trading businesses and many international oil companies running oil rigs off the coast.

Workers were attracted to the region from neighbouring countries including Mali, Niger and Senegal. Then, due to a decline in oil prices and cheaper sites being discovered elsewhere, the unstable economic climate caused tensions to mount. Racial discrimination and violence became more flagrant, reports of attacks on expatriates started circulating and for the first time I became overly conscious of the colour of my skin.

It seems that both projection and blame come very much to the fore when humans are faced with hardship. Whilst the Ivorian community was happy to accommodate expatriate visitors when the country was financially stable, economic decline caused them to radically change their perception. Both prejudice and racism appear to be largely driven by suffering or discomfort, the desire to attribute blame to an external party or group, and the projection that is created as a result. Evidently, it is not reality that fuels and drives hatred, prejudice and discrimination, it is misunderstanding and pain.

Prejudice is all-pervasive and exists in all cultures, families, classrooms, teams, workplaces and religions. Racism is one type of prejudice. Our understanding of projection and humankind's willingness to attribute blame can lead us to a better grasp of the problem and with a bit of luck, help us devise some useful strategies for overcoming the problems that ultimately lead to conflict on a global scale.

"Poverty is the worst form of violence"

Mahatma Gandhi

Jealousy: *The Lose/Lose Emotion*

"If you love someone, set them free. If they come back they're yours;
if they don't they never were"

Richard Bach

Cambridge Dictionary:

Jealousy – a feeling of unhappiness and anger because someone has something or someone that you want.

Envy – to wish that you had something that another person has.

When my schoolmates were being cruel and unkind in primary school, I would ask myself and my parents why it was so. My parents would tell me not to worry, it was probably jealousy. This confused me no end, as my self-esteem was so very low and the picture of myself I held in my head was so very small and insignificant, I couldn't for the life of me imagine why anyone would be jealous.

It rarely helps a child who feels insecure to hear that people are jealous of them. When well-meaning parents or friends shrug off bullying as jealousy, it can feel like a platitude or worse, an attempt

"Knowing what's right doesn't mean much unless you do what's right"

Theodore Roosevelt

to distract you from the fact you are worthless and insignificant. Jealousy is not experienced by everyone to the same degree. People who have an inner focus, the daydreamers and the creative spirits who are often the victims of bullying, may not experience jealousy, so it can be a difficult emotion to understand and very tricky to spot in others.

Envy is a longing for something or a desire, as opposed to jealousy which is more of a hostile, possessive emotion. It is possible to be envious of another person without wishing them any ill. Jealousy, however, is a fear or anger based emotion and is aggressive. Through shame, jealously is often repressed or hidden so it can be very difficult to spot in another and equally difficult to respond to.

Feelings of jealousy drive many people to destructive and harmful behaviours, particularly in close relationships. This can cause disastrous consequences when left unchecked. A great deal of domestic violence can be attributed to jealousy and possessiveness stemming from low confidence and self-esteem.

If you find yourself involved with a jealous or possessive person you will probably find it impossible to satisfy their demands. No amount of negotiation or rule setting will give them peace of mind. If you attempt to modify your behaviour to appease them, you will find yourself on a long, arduous and fruitless search for harmony. If you do modify your behaviour to please them for the sake of peace, you will undoubtedly find yourself faced with new and more imposing demands over time.

In my early 20s my then boyfriend insisted I place all the beautiful gifts and expensive jewellery from my previous relationship into a box and throw it into the river. I felt very disturbed by this and although I didn't mind at all giving away the jewellery, I did mind sending it to the bottom of a river where it would be of benefit to no one.

I acquiesced, but as a consequence my feelings about him changed. I lost respect for his decision-making and, as I had suspected all along, my gesture did not heal or remove his insecurities. It did not bring me the peace I hoped for in the relationship and remains to this day a moment I regret.

"This above all: to thine own self be true. And it must follow, as the night the day. Thou canst not then be false to any man"

William Shakespeare

In schools, jealousy shows up as one child insisting their friend play *only* with them and not the other children. It is important to help your children stand their ground and not allow them to be coerced into exclusivity, neglecting or rejecting friends as a placation to an alpha male or female. Pushing another child into exclusivity is a power play, so help your child understand that this is not okay and can seriously hurt or demoralise the people who find themselves excluded or rejected.

Refusing to give in to the demands of a jealous and possessive friend is the kindest and healthiest action you can take. In intimate relationships, it is important to stand firm if your partner has demands that inhibit you or are an imposition and contrary to your wishes. Whatever concessions you make on your happiness today, you will have to live with the consequences for a very long time.

"There are no good excuses for bad behaviour"

Fear, jealousy and the consequent anger are responsible for a large number of relationship conflicts and can be truly and catastrophically toxic. The person who is feeling fearful, angry or jealous will *never* be appeased by the actions of another, because those feelings are always present regardless of what is happening around them. The feelings they are experiencing are as a result of their projections, their filters and their interpretation of the world.

There is literally nothing that you can do to help if you are in relationship with a jealous and insecure bully. At best you can hope for a temporary calm and a short peaceful period until the next trigger happens. You will also *never* be able to pre-empt the next trigger because the bully will change the rules all the time and have myriad reasons why this is logical and acceptable behaviour.

As generally people don't choose to consider the root cause of their feelings of jealousy and insecurity, they inevitably blame those who surround them and see others as the instigators and cause of all dramas and upsets in their life. Responsibility for jealousy and possessiveness lies squarely and 100% with the person who is feeling the emotions. They and they alone hold the solution to the problem. Feelings of jealousy originate from a jealous and possessive mind. Jealousy as an emotion has nothing to do with truth or external reality, and the victim or object of their attention has little or no power to help them.

Coaching or therapy will help, but only if the person who is experiencing the jealousy chooses to seek help. If they are pushed or coerced into a therapeutic solution, it is unlikely that they will be invested in the process and as such, unlikely to get results.

Healing is an internal process of change that needs to be undertaken by the person experiencing the negative and destructive emotions. In order for a jealous and possessive person to gain a sense of balance, they need to seek help or guidance from outside of the relationship, assume responsibility for their emotional state and take control of the behaviour themselves.

"Look well into thyself; there is a source of strength which will always spring up if thou wilt always look there"

Marcus Aurelius

SECTION 2

THE DIFFERENT FACES OF BULLYING

Frenemies - *When Friends or Family Attack*

"An insincere and evil friend is more to be feared than a wild beast; a wild beast may wound your body, but an evil friend will wound your mind"

Buddha

There are people in the world who see problems in everything, the worst in everyone and on the whole, feel that the world is a hostile place and against them. Let's call them *frenemies*. Often these people feel like the world owes them and they deserve better. They are obsessive, have a strong tendency to dwell on past problems and see the glass as eternally half empty.

This type of thinking can be well installed and operating in even the youngest of children. As they age, frenemies become more and more disillusioned as they realise that their ailments, the economy, government, neighbour etc. are as bad as ever and the knight in shining armour/princess/lottery ticket has not shown up to rescue them.

Frenemies are people who appear to be your friend or ally but secretly are jealous, distrustful and negative, and harbour ill will towards you *at this present moment in time*. People are *not* their behaviour, and human beings have an infinite capacity for change. Your friend and ally today could easily transform into an indifferent or bitter adversary just as an adversary could transform into a close and loving friend. Life is funny like that.

There may be someone in your world who on the surface appears to be your friend but you feel uncertain about them and sometimes wonder whether they like you at all. People do not always authentically represent themselves and so, even with

"Some people find fault like there is a reward for it"

Zig Ziglar

knowledge and experience, it is hard to recognise a frenemy. Most people are worth giving the benefit of the doubt, but if you are unsure, check this list for characteristics to look out for:

- ❀ Complains about almost everything and everybody
- ❀ Attracted to gossip, drama and problems
- ❀ See themselves as victims and feel badly done by
- ❀ See themselves as the unlucky ones, the black sheep, and can be often heard to say, "If it wasn't for the government, economy, ailment, weather, neighbour, childhood, upbringing, parents, school life, immigrants, etc., life would be fine"
- ❀ Often have a 'lottery' or 'princess in the tower' mentality, clinging to the idea that something is going to happen to bring them happiness with little or no effort on their part
- ❀ Feel they have somehow missed out, been overlooked or ignored
- ❀ Feel that people who achieve success are lucky and undeserving
- ❀ Rarely if ever apologise or see themselves at fault

Ironically, frenemies can be incredibly friendly and charismatic, generous to a fault, kind, considerate and helpful. In a frenemy however, the loving and kind aspect of themselves is conditional and depends on you being willing to accept hostility and abuse as part of the package deal.

"Great minds discuss ideas; average minds discuss events; small minds discuss people"

Eleanor Roosevelt

A frenemy rarely, if ever, accepts that they are at fault in a situation. Apologies are a scarce and sometimes unheard-of commodity and problems will be swept under the carpet to be left as a dark harbour of ill feeling. In these circumstances it is almost impossible to experience growth and development and can lead to long term degeneration of the relationship. Many a frenemy has gone to the grave without resolving or addressing issues. The more easily you recognise this pattern, the more likely you are to take action to avoid the repercussions.

Relationships where unreasonable behaviours are ignored and left unspoken and unrecognised, will remain stuck in a painful cycle. Healthy relationships inevitably face highs and lows, conflict and resolution, friction and peace. Problems take on greater significance and create unnecessary strain when the conflict has no resolution, the friction is not soothed by ensuing peace and harmony, and the highs are heavily outnumbered by the lows.

Frenemies can and do cause great damage to the people around them. They will attempt to bring you down if they suspect you don't agree with them and are exceedingly inclined to bully. If you are in a relationship with someone like this, either at school, at work or in the home, then you will need plenty of tools and techniques to co-exist peacefully.

The Strategy

Beware of the seduction of talking about others in derogatory and hurtful ways, as someone who is in the habit of speaking badly about another will not think twice before turning you into the next topic for annihilation. More

"Be kind whenever possible.

It is always possible"

Dalai Lama

importantly, you are contributing to a big dark pool of emotional pollution that will not go unnoticed. Be mindful of the energetic connection that exists between all beings, whether conscious or unconscious.

Be kind and generous of spirit when discussing others. A rule of thumb could be, if you are speaking of another, make sure that what you say is in line with your beliefs and values. If you were in a discussion with the person you are speaking of, you should be happy to repeat what you are saying, to them directly.

It is wiser to focus on your own judgement, your sense of self-worth and your internal guidance system if you are to find comfort and serenity in this uncertain world. Ultimately you will never truly know how deep your friendships or family ties run. Those who do not reveal themselves, may be hostile, may be indifferent or may be friendly. Either way, it need not concern you. Treat all people with love and respect. The rest is in their hands.

The Family

If the description of a frenemy applies to a close family member, it is probable that your life will be uncomfortable and perhaps at times, acutely painful. We are naturally inclined to gauge our sense of value and worth from those around us, especially during our formative years. It can be extremely challenging to live with someone who sees, energises and brings forth the worst in you.

This can be the most demoralising and difficult form of bullying and if you find yourself in this situation you will need to be especially vigilant and take great care not to find yourself adopting a false and negative sense of self based on their perception.

In truth, all of us have good, bad and mediocre aspects of ourselves. We all possess the ability to be kind and hurtful, strong and weak, happy and sad, to succeed and to fail. If you live close to someone whose focus and attention is placed on the negative aspects of you, it can be tremendously difficult to see yourself in a positive light.

"Exact numbers aren't needed to realise that we spend too much time with those who poison us with pessimism, sloth, and low expectations of themselves and the world. It is often the case that you have to fire certain friends or retire from particular social circles to have the life you want. This isn't being mean; it is being practical. Poisonous people do not deserve your time. To think otherwise is masochistic."

Timothy Ferriss
'The Four Hour Work Week'

"Reality is entirely subjective. Each person has a different understanding of truth. There is no ultimate reality, only reality as we see it"

If you do have such a person (or persons) in your family, be conscious of how you spend your time, what discussions you are willing to participate in and, if possible, limit your interactions. These situations are inevitably fraught with complex loyalties and family considerations which can be out of your control. At times walking away from the problem is not possible, at least not in the short term. If you find yourself exposed to this kind of personality type and behaviour, focus on maintaining a healthy sense of self in amongst the hostilities. Although it is difficult and at times painful, it is possible.

In certain situations, relationships can deteriorate so badly that they are no longer viable and peace can only be achieved once the parties have moved well away from each other. Family ruptures such as these can have far-reaching consequences and be difficult to manage; however, in certain circumstances, the ending of some relationships is inevitable and ultimately, unavoidable. Sometimes self-preservation, health and well-being, and a clear understanding that an abusive, hostile and controlling personality will not cede ground enough to make the relationship work, may have to override a sense of family loyalty. Decisions like these should not be taken lightly as many people will be affected.

Family rifts are distressing on many levels and if not managed well, will cause a continual drain on your emotions and energy. If you are involved in conflict of this kind, use the seven-step programme later in the book to support you on your journey back to peaceful personal power. In cases where there is a great deal of emotional distress it is advisable to pay particular attention to the forgiveness and meditation practices.

"The weak can never forgive. Forgiveness is the attribute of the strong"

Mahatma Gandhi

Why Can't You See Me?

"In the end, we will remember not the words of our enemies, but the silence of our friends"

Martin Luther King, Jr.

I have had the deep misfortune, or fortune, depending on your point of view, of experiencing such a person with fairly catastrophic results. A person within my extended family circle took a dramatic and obvious dislike to me. Let's call her Madeline. Being only in my 20s at the time, I felt very lost and confused by the hostility. Although I had at that time experienced my fair share of bullying and intimidation, I had not until then experienced it with such an obvious intensity and from someone who had such close access to me nor from someone who, in my humble opinion, should have seen me as being a relatively peaceful person worthy of respect.

My solution at the time was to do my very best to accommodate her behaviour, hoping to show her that I was a trustworthy, valuable and loving person. I chose to forgive her lack of courtesy and kindness and ceded ground as much as possible with the vain hope that she would see the error of her ways. This, of course, did not work. The relationship limped along in bad shape for several years with a great deal of angst along the way until one day I received a very painful and very hurtful letter. Up to that point, although I knew in no uncertain terms that she was not my biggest fan, I was completely unprepared for the frenzied and hate-filled tirade that ensued.

"To understand someone well, pay attention to their opinion of others"

In the letter I was described in the ugliest of terms and the ugliest of ways. It was a great shock and I felt nauseous and disoriented for quite some time afterwards. As I was so young and unfamiliar with this type of behaviour and also unaware that it is possible to let go of such things with ease, it took me a great deal of time to recover from my sadness, surprise, hurt and disappointment. That letter played through my mind for a good 18 months afterwards and every time I thought of it I felt ill.

Until that point in time I had assumed that fundamentally most people either liked or were indifferent to me. I had never experienced such overt and unbridled anger and hatred nor observed it in any family I had been connected to. Eventually, after a while I recovered my composure and discovered something very interesting about myself. That I could be hated and despised and still manage to feel okay.

"Do what you feel in your heart to be right — for you'll be criticised anyway"

Eleanor Roosevelt

I intentionally chose to memorise the words in the letter, as they have become one of my greatest gifts and within them lies a great lesson. This experience has taught me that no matter how hard I try, how much I do, how willing I am to make concessions, there are people in the world who just don't get me, who *really* don't like me and don't wish to be friends with me. There is great freedom in that knowledge.

At 40 something, I now love the fact I received that message. I love the fact that someone tried so very hard to hurt me and to bring me down that I stepped out of people-pleasing, stepped out of wishing for approval and stepped into my personal power. It has given me the gift of myself and the freedom that until then I had not allowed myself. I no longer need to receive the *approval* of others. Take me or leave me, like me, love me or not, I will always be open to friendship and withdraw from hostility and hurt without a second thought. You know what people say about opinions...

It has also been said that time heals all wounds. As it turns out, Madeline developed a chronic pattern of conflict with many family members and friends and had consequently a long list of broken relationships in her wake;

"In the practice of tolerance, one's enemy is the best teacher"

Dalai Lama

none of which, of course, she felt personally responsible for. Personality types with excessive demands and volatile behaviours are extremely difficult to manage within a family unit at the best of times. If you find yourself in this situation it is wise to seek advice from trusted friends or professional support if necessary.

What I did walk away with was a deeper understanding of the divide that can exist between two people's thinking and the conclusion that you can please some of the people some of the time, but you invariably cannot please all of the people all of the time. I realised that sometimes you have to stop ceding ground and instead concede defeat. I learned that some relationships are unsalvageable and in some circumstances your energy is better spent elsewhere. We are all worthy of love and compassion. Choose the company you keep wisely, and how you spend your time and energy with intention.

If you find yourself with someone like this in your life, be conscious of what you are willing to share about yourself as anything you do say is open to distortion and misinterpretation. Limit your time together as best you can and privately wish them all the best. Be mindful of the need to balance yourself with meditation, space-clearing and forgiveness rituals. Negative thinking attracts negative experience and as such is a self-fulfilling prophecy. It is not your job to teach people that angry and destructive behaviour will bring them pain and suffering. That lesson they may well have to learn on their own.

"It's not your job to like me, it's mine"

Byron Katie

When family or close friends bully you it is very easy to believe what they have to say about you and sometimes difficult to find your true sense of self. It is easy at these times to become lost and downhearted. Their perception of you is a reflection of them, so don't take it to heart.

"I don't have to be what you want me to be"

Muhammad Ali

Hidden in the Dark - *Amanda's Story*

*"If you want to see the brave,
look at those who can forgive"*

Bhagavad Gita

It can be difficult to make the association between domestic abuse and bullying and on the other hand, as Dr Gandhi has so eloquently pointed out, evidence suggests that some children readily accept anger, dominance, abusive behaviour and at times, violence, as a normal and reasonable fact of life.

If this is the case, where did they learn that to be so? What is going awry in our cultural story that families are suffering under the false imagining that tempers are unalterable and behaviour impossible to modify? This story illustrates the reality of an existence that many people live, but few are willing to admit to. If we can at least remove the stigma and embarrassment that surrounds the spectre of homes that are governed by the inability of people to control or manage their tempers, then we have started an important dialogue.

The light flickered in the fireplace and the shadows danced ominously. I was hiding, tucked away in the corner next to the bed and was very, very afraid. I couldn't hear a sound from the rest of the house and that scared me all the more. Was she okay? Where was he? What was going on? Should I run, should I stay, should I try and make it to the telephone in the kitchen? No, I daren't do that. I was on the ground floor, near the front door. Perhaps leaving was an option? Was I in danger?

Why does fear do this to me? Why does it take away my ability to think straight? Where are my survival instincts when I need them most?

We had only been in my in-laws' house for a short time and they had until this moment acted like normal, everyday people with a normal, everyday life. How could I have been so blind, so stupid to what was lurking beneath the veneer of normalcy? How do people hide this kind of stuff from the world? I had only recently been inducted into this new and unusual family. I tried to look at my watch but it was too dark and I was afraid to put the light on and risk drawing attention to myself.

Ryan and I were staying with his parents for a few weeks and he was working nights. It was **supposed** to be a nice thing to do. It was **supposed** to be my opportunity to really get to know them and feel included as a new family member, given I was so very far away from all that I knew and loved. Yet there I was, hiding in the dark on my own, too afraid to move, while some kind of mad, alternate universe spun around me. This wasn't **supposed** to be happening.

A sharp tapping at the window abruptly took me from my self-pitying thoughts but I was almost too petrified to look. The tapping became more insistent and I reluctantly gave up my dark nook to investigate. It was Ryan's mother, outside in the darkness and the snow. Her jumper had been somehow pulled off her back and she was shivering in her flimsy thermal singlet as she climbed into the bedroom. Then we saw the flashlight…

It ended quietly. His mother stood silently watching through the window as the flashlight pan around in the inky darkness for a short while. She took a deep breath, looked over at me, walked out the door and closed it noiselessly behind her. I stayed, curled in a little ball, hiding between the bed and the fireplace, staying as quiet and as invisible as I could and praying for the quick return of Ryan. There were no more sounds, the house remained ominously silent as a grave.

The next morning we found remnants of burnt wooden artefacts in the front room. I imagine they were the couple's mementoes or reminders of happier times. Water had been poured on the floor, perhaps to put out the remains of the smouldering timber. That morning we packed our bags and left.

After that night, my understanding of family was forever altered. What I had hoped for as I embarked on my journey into this new group of people fell apart and blew away in the icy wind. The friendship, the trust, the loyalty and the naive belief that families take care of each other, protect each other, respect each other and provide safe harbour in a storm.

> "Life is not the way it's supposed to be. It's the way it is. The way you cope with it is what makes the difference"
>
> Virginia Satir

It took me many years to make sense of that night, and many more to make sense of the turmoil and conflict that followed. Today, I find myself at peace with it all.

I have now come to understand that the real

problem I faced was not the events of the night itself, it was the naivety that led me to sit vulnerable and alone in a house where I was clearly at risk. My situation could have been easily remedied; at the first sign of trauma I could have run to the local police station or a neighbour's house and phoned Ryan or nearby family members. I could have grabbed my bags and headed for the airport, or any number of alternative solutions. My problem wasn't the drama that unfolded around me, my problem was my inability to make good decisions when faced with a bad situation. My problem was me.

It is many years since I forgave Ryan's father for his behaviour. It was never spoken of again and as such I had to find my own way of resolving the problem. My learnings all came from a strong desire to

"What the caterpillar calls the end of the world the master calls a butterfly"

Richard Bach

let go of the past and move on with my life. Hostility, vengefulness and anger are emotions that don't sit well with me. I do my best to accommodate people where I can, will reach out if I think I can be of service, but when my well-being and/or safety are compromised, or I am having no impact on the situation, then it's time to re-evaluate the relationship.

Without doubt, I now consider this experience to be a huge blessing. It opened my eyes to a world I had until then not imagined to be real. It gave me an opportunity to see brutality, dominance and anger-based relationships at work and discover how and why they remain intact. It gave me a deeper understanding into the turmoil that raged in my husband and an insight into how to help him. It gave me an opportunity to reconsider my position within the family, draw my own conclusions about anger-based relationships and ultimately, it gave me the desire to share my story in this book.

I have to thank my father-in-law for all he has done for me. He has given the gift of experience and for that, I will be forever grateful.

"Every problem has a gift for you in its hands"

Richard Bach

From Bullied to Bully - *Ryan's Story*

"Mistakes are always forgivable,
if one has the courage to admit them"

Bruce Lee

*I*was very young when I first realised I was scared of my father. I
would wait on Friday nights to hear whether he put the key in
the front door or whether he banged with his fist. If he used the key
I could relax and go to sleep. If he rang the doorbell loudly I would
crawl under my bed and hide. I knew Mum would be in for it.

I don't want to talk much about those times. It doesn't help to
dwell on it. I just remember that I was very scared. When I was in
the car with him I would always leave my hand sitting on the door
handle, just in case…

A serious and reserved man, my father worked hard during the
week and would head down to the pub with his mates every Friday
afternoon. His major shortcoming was an inability to manage his
volatile temper. He was physically strong, and terrifying when he
allowed himself to fall into a rage. This created great turmoil for
me, being the only son and particularly protective of Mum, who
was very gentle and soft.

My grandmother explained away my father's uncontrolled
behaviour as due to his Irish temper, so when I acted the same
way, it was accepted as inevitable in my family. Sometimes I tried
to help Mum but I was so young and so small, it just made things
worse. I made up for it in the playground at school. I couldn't stand
bullying, so I would get involved in any problem that came up and
defend the person being picked on. It felt good to be able to help
someone like that.

At the time I saw myself as a defender of the weak, able to stop
the abusers in a way I had been unable to do at home. But I always
felt terrible after I won a fight and most of the time I would cry
when I realised I had hurt them. I would feel their pain. I didn't
understand; fighting the bullies was supposed to make me feel
better but really it was the opposite.

I had my last fight when I was still fairly young and impetuous. After an altercation in a club where I was supposedly defending my girlfriend's honour, I looked down on the guy I had hurt, saw the pain in his eyes and realised I was no better than him. A bully masquerading as a hero, but a bully even so.

"An eye for an eye makes the whole world go blind"

Mahatma Gandhi

It was then that I realised what I had become. All those years I thought I was defending the weak, when really I was a bully just like the rest of them. I never hit another person again.

I grew up and married. The relationship with my father remained turbulent. I had no self-esteem or confidence when I was around him and easily became caught up in his way of thinking, adopting his pattern of controlling jealousy and anger. All this I found difficult to keep from my wife and son, which eventually caused me to hit a turning point in my life.

I had an argument with Amanda, triggered and fuelled by feelings that were stirred up from being around my father. In the heat of the moment I picked up a chair, held it over my head and gestured as if I was going to launch it through the window over her and my son's heads. It was as if time stood still. I stopped and looked at my boy, flashing back to childhood images of my own father using violence and anger in our home.

As I looked at my son's face, I realised with shock that I was allowing myself to become a tyrant in my own family, the one thing I had hated growing up and sworn I never ever wanted to be. I put the chair down slowly and left. I drove for some time, parked the car in front of a river and cried as I thought of the look on the faces of the two most important people in my life and how much I had frightened them.

I wondered how I could help my son, or if I would ever have his forgiveness. I knew this experience would have a huge impact on him in the same way my father's behaviour had impacted on me as a child. I had wanted a son so badly. I had wanted to give him everything I missed out on in my relationship with my dad, but here I was, on the verge of ruining it all and losing both him and my wife.

"Forgiveness says you are given another chance to make a new beginning"

Desmond Tutu

That moment completely changed my life and taught me my biggest lesson. My focus turned away from my father and towards personal responsibility. I stopped blaming my past, my father, my genetics and my childhood and focused instead on protecting my family and learning how to deal with my anger and rage. Instead of running from the challenge and blaming my upbringing as I had done my whole life, I decided to face it like a man.

Thirteen years on from that day, we are well and truly on the other side. I did everything in my power to make amends and made sure everyone was free to speak and share their feelings about what happened. I now have an honest and loving relationship with my son, who was gracious enough to forgive me for scaring him and his mother, and I have taken an interesting journey of discovery to learn how to let go of my anger.

My loving and ever-patient wife Amanda is thankfully still at my side and continues to help me examine the complexities of my upbringing and how they affected me as a man. My father, sadly, remained a troubled man until his death, although we thankfully made peace with each other at the end.

I am grateful to my father. Through him I have learned that we are able to take control of ourselves and our future. I have learned that we are not victims of circumstance and that we have the power to change even the most deep-seated patterns if we choose to. Because of my father, I have learned how to become a better man.

*"If you think you're enlightened,
go spend a week with your family"*

Ram Dass

When Friends Turn Away

*"Old friends pass away, new friends appear. It is just like the days.
An old day passes, a new day arrives. The important thing is to
make it meaningful: a meaningful friend—or a meaningful day"*

Dalai Lama

There is another less known phenomenon that can be interpreted as a form of bullying. There are times in life when you change direction, make significant lifestyle changes, become busier, change career, take up a new hobby or sport, join a new club or experience a relationship breakdown. At times like these you can feel overwhelmed, uncertain and look for reassurance in your family or friendship circle.

At these times you may notice that instead of being enthusiastic and encouraging, some of your close friends and family become unusually quiet, withdrawn and strangely disinterested in you. At the time it can feel like a passive-aggressive attack and can leave you feeling bereft and alone. When you learn a new skill, meet a new partner or reach out for new horizons, the people who are closest to you often become confused by the changes and uncertain as to whether they approve or not. Human beings are notable for being uncomfortable with change, including the changes they witness in friends and family.

This transition can have a profound effect on your immediate relationships. When this happens, there is a great need to focus your thoughts, breathe deep, and develop a slightly thicker skin. Give them time to adjust to and accept the transformation they are seeing in you.

> *"Even if you are a minority of one, the truth is the truth"*
>
> Mohandas Gandhi

There are many reasons for people to withdraw; sometimes all they need is a little time to see that everything is going to be okay.

As you transition to the updated, revamped and revised version of you, although you may possibly feel lonely and rejected, be aware that you will inevitably attract new people into your world who will be more aligned with your new way of thinking. The transition will undoubtedly require much of your time and attention which will soften the effects of losing the support of those you love and cherish. The period of loneliness does not need to last long if you focus on what you want instead of what you don't want.

True friends and loving family will come back to you in their own time. The others, well, bless the moments you shared together and be grateful for the space you now have in your life to welcome and create something new.

As part of your growth and evolution it is important to allow some space for old friendships to end and new friendships to come in. As we grow and develop as individuals, not only do our likes and dislikes shift and change but also our relationships and friendships. Change is inevitable, growth is not. In order to be able to develop into the next best version of yourself, shift your focus from *why* to *what next* and embrace change with gusto and enthusiasm.

Never trade your dreams for comfort or companionship. Life is for living, not for biding time and it is entirely possible to follow your dreams whilst remaining committed and close to your immediate family and friends. You may find yourself bewildered and misunderstood at times, you may have your intellect or sanity questioned. But if you are following *your* dreams doesn't it make sense that few can see where you are going or understand how you are going to get there?

"I have learned that success is to be measured not so much by the position that one has reached in life as by the obstacles which he has had to overcome while trying to succeed"

Booker T. Washington

Playing to the Crowd

"It's like deja-vu, all over again"

Yogi Berra

Whilst working as a flight attendant I observed an interesting aspect of group behaviour. When travelling alone or in small groups, passengers are in general calm and accommodating in their behaviour. The odd person may have a bad day and be short tempered and difficult, however the majority of travellers are either obliging or indifferent. Groups however, are a completely different kettle of fish.

School groups are inevitably raucous and excited, but behaviour is generally well monitored by the accompanying teachers. Professional sports teams are on the whole the best behaved of the groups, which is probably a consequence of them being highly disciplined along with travelling a great deal. The ones to look out for are groups of friends going or coming back from some special occasion or holiday. As a flight attendant you become the obvious target of the alpha member of the group and inevitably find yourself dealing with raucous, flirtatious or disruptive behaviour.

What I found interesting about this was that if you had the very same passengers on the very same trip, travelling alone or in twos, you would not experience the same kind of behaviour. The smaller groups of passengers would never cause disruptions unless they were heavily intoxicated.

Passengers in larger groups are far more rowdy and likely to engage in banter with the flight attendant. Evidently, people who would usually be reluctant to engage in conversation, draw their strength in numbers and enjoy playing to a crowd.

Handling groups is a challenge for adults and children alike, and bullying sometimes occurs as a crowd pleaser or demonstration of power. When you come across someone who is playing to the crowd at your expense, do your best to remove yourself from the situation as quickly as possible and take much of what they say with a pinch of salt.

"People seldom do what they believe in.
They do what is convenient, then repent"

Bob Dylan

Homophobia

"The bullying was hideous and relentless, and we turned it round by making ourselves celebrities"

Julian Clary

Oxford Dictionary:

Homophobia – *An extreme and irrational aversion to homosexuality and homosexual people.*

Homophobia encompasses all negative attitudes, biases and behaviours towards the gay, lesbian, bisexual and transgender communities. The FBI Annual Hate Crimes Statistics for 2011 noted that 20.8% of hate crimes resulted from sexual orientation bias. Like all other prejudices, homophobia is senseless and misguided. It is saddening to know that in some countries it is illegal to be homosexual or engage in homosexual activity.

High schoolers are particularly vulnerable to peer pressure, prejudice and bigotry, as they are in a demanding transitional developmental stage. Socially, school is challenging for any teen to navigate but it can be exceptionally tough for minority groups, and as such homophobic bullying has been identified as a potential driver for teen suicides. Strong mentoring and support is critical to help these young people transition into powerful, optimistic, creative and valued members of society.

The need for community love and tolerance has never been greater. Regardless of your stance on homosexuality, exceptional kindness and tolerance is required for all young people who find themselves in this rapid and confusing period of self-discovery. Many young people are suffering unnecessarily as a result of the stigma and shame that surrounds sexual orientation. It is our duty as a loving community to ensure that this kind of bigotry no long poses a threat to our youth.

"The highest result of education is tolerance"

Helen Keller

"This is my simple religion. There is no need for temples; no need for complicated philosophy. Our own brain, our own heart is our temple; the philosophy is kindness"

Dalai Lama

Cyber Bullying

"It has become appallingly obvious that our technology has exceeded our humanity"

Albert Einstein

Technology has both dramatically improved and dramatically complicated life as we know it. No longer are we able to shield and protect our children from the world. It is becoming increasingly difficult for parents to safely monitor and patrol what children are exposed to through the media and social interaction. If you do manage to shield your child through primary school (and I would be very surprised if in this day and age you succeed), once they are at high school even the illusion of control disappears in a demoralising puff of smoke. Bar home schooling, there is no way to guarantee your child does not come into contact with material that would be unheard of and almost impossible for a child to access only a few years ago.

Children's absorption in a virtual reality is compounded by the disconnect from parents in this fast-paced and over-stimulated world. Increased pressures on parents juggling work and home responsibilities create a parental void that children are filling with online games and social media conversations.

An imbalanced dependence on virtual relationships can sabotage normal family interactions if left unchecked. Some children rely heavily on a network of online friends for entertainment, advice and guidance, which opens up potential problems. This community can become manipulative, destructive and damaging without the wisdom, temperance and love of an adult, and our children are left blowing in the chilly cyber wind.

Social media and mobile phones can be used intentionally to cause pain and trauma, and also unintentionally through the thoughtlessness that accompanies the teenage years. There have been some tragic cases of young people taking their lives due to the insensitivity of others.

Anything that goes on social media *stays* there and is at *all* times open to misuse by others. If you delete a post on social media it remains traceable and can ultimately be used against you legally or to discredit you many years afterwards. A strong sense of self-control and social responsibility is needed when posting photos or sensitive content. In many states and countries cyber bullying is also punishable by law and as such it is wise to err on the side of caution if you intend to post material designed to intimidate or embarrass another. As a rule, do not photograph or video yourself or any person in a compromising situation or in a way that may attract unwanted attention. Do not make threats against another, even in jest, nor take, promote or be party to compromising or hurtful material.

"I got made fun of constantly in high school. That's what built my character. That's what makes you who you are. When you get made fun of, when people point out your weaknesses, that's just another opportunity for you to rise above"

Zac Efron

If you have a strong and supportive online community, any kind of cyber bullying or abuse can be dealt with swiftly and the power of the herd will see that it goes no further.

If you, however, are a lone voice with little or no support, it is much easier for aggressive, manipulative or hostile parties to cause problems. Scores of people have been duped by online connections. Many have lost money, some have lost so much more. The grooming of young people by paedophiles and con artists is prevalent and dangerous, and there are tragic stories of stalkers befriending and luring vulnerable people with sometimes unspeakable consequences.

With this gloomy, disempowering and somewhat depressing knowledge, we need to wake up to the fact that a deepened understanding of the technology available to our children is required if we are to offer them protection. Like it or not, responsible parenting requires that we learn about the technology that surrounds us.

To support your child with social media, become familiar with the networks they intend to use and become involved yourself. Become Facebook 'friends' with your children as a condition of use, and make your expectations of online behaviour clear. You are not being respectful of their space by staying out of your child's virtual world. The online world is not a place for privacy; it is a public domain and should be considered as such to avoid problems.

To help keep the flow of conversation happening in your home, turn off electronics at designated times, such as meal times. Make sure you talk with your children regularly about things that matter and keep dialogue open so that they feel safe sharing their problems with you.

Most of all, recognise the power of the *Delete, Report and Block* functions on phones and social media sites, and also the law enforcement options should it reach that stage. You have the power and the ability to remove and report people from your virtual world. It serves no purpose to remain in contact with people whose intention is to cause you distress or harm. You are responsible for who you allow into your personal and virtual space and you are equally responsible for moving away from them if necessary.

Banning your child from having access to social media is not an option unless you feel yourself to be a parent with absolute power over your child. There are countless ways a young person can outwit, outplay and outlast their parents if they are desperate to have a private social media world. Teaching your teenagers to be transparent and open, to share their virtual life with the people who care for them, eliminates much of the insidiousness of social media. Social media, when used correctly, can be great fun and highly entertaining when treated as a public domain, assuming any and all material published there is fit for any member of your family to see, including Nana.

Establishing some good ground rules for social media with your children can help as they progress into the world of teenage independence and move away from parental control. If they understand the basic principles of social media interaction and the need to behave with responsibility and integrity, and if you have a relationship based on trust and mutual respect, then the rest is up to them.

Used with caution, discretion, sensitivity and sense social media can be a fantastic resource and powerful means of communication. Use it wisely and use it well with the understanding that your presence there is being recorded. Besides, Nana is watching.

> *"Stay away from people who gossip and spread rumours. They are choosing the path of emotional bullying and negativity"*
>
> Steve Maraboli

"You can observe a lot by just watching"

Yogi Berra

No Kidding - *Yvette Adams*

"Learn from yesterday, live for today, hope for tomorrow. The important thing is not to stop questioning"

Albert Einstein

Yvette Adams is a serial entrepreneur currently running three businesses: The Creative Collective, The Training Collective, and Awardshub. A speaker, blogger and author, she is regularly called on by media on technology related topics.

Yvette published her second book, *'No Kidding—Why our kids know more about technology than us and what we can do about it'* in 2014.

> *Our generation of parents has a great responsibility in the digital age. Not just because we want to be the best parents we can be and we're struggling with what that means with technology involved, but because we are the generation that bridges the memory of life before technology and a life that is full of technology.*
>
> *The task is an onerous one. If we do a good job, the world will be our children's oyster, opening opportunities which never existed before. If we choose to ignore technology, and tell our kids they can't use social networks or technology for play or for work, and if we don't make time to take an active interest in what our kids are actually doing online, the ramifications can be disastrous.*
>
> *That's just the beginning of the challenge we're presented with in parenting in these times of rapid change and information overload. Our children are dealing with safety and privacy concerns we never had to contend with, and are creating giant digital footprints. Our education system hasn't caught up and we are attempting to prepare them for jobs that don't exist yet.*
>
> *So what are the key questions you, as a parent who cares, need to ask your children? What do you need to do to ensure cyber safety and minimise cyber bullying?*

I recommend a Family Technology Charter—a written agreement between family members regarding issues such as technology ownership, use, control and employment. The Family Technology Charter articulates the values of your family in regards to technology and sets a framework for making some important decisions. Every family is different, as should be your Family Technology Charter.

The process of developing a Family Technology Charter is powerful because it gives everyone a say in the matter, whatever their age and ability with technology, and can facilitate some healthy discussions. It can also minimise family conflicts by clearly laying out the 'rules of the road' before problems arise. So it becomes a handy reference point when dramas do happen!

Some discussion points to help you create your own Family Technology Charter:

1. Set appropriate amounts of time to be on technology per day

CONSIDERATIONS: Is there a set amount of time that technology can and can't be used? Different guidelines are provided by different authorities on appropriate time limits per day for appropriate age groups. Only three out of ten kids say that their parents set limits on their media use and stick to them, according to the 2010 study Generation M2: Media in the Lives of 8 to 18-Year-Olds, conducted by the Kaiser Family Foundation.

EXAMPLE: All technology can only be used for two hours per day.

2. Technology curfews

CONSIDERATIONS: Are there set times that technology can be used in your family? For instance, must phones, computers and gaming devices be turned off during meals? Must they be turned off by 8pm each week night? What about on weekends and school holidays? Can they go on it before school? How will you enforce the curfew? Will devices need to be handed into a central location by a set time to ensure no undercover use into the wee hours?

EXAMPLE: All technology must be switched off by 8pm on week nights and handed into the designated technology basket in the kitchen. All technology must be switched off and handed in by 9pm on weekends and school holidays.

3. Location of use

CONSIDERATIONS: Are there set locations that technology can and can't be used? Some families require that computers and smart phones be used in public spaces and charged in a central area—like the kitchen. In addition to removing the temptation for kids, it gives you an opportunity to randomly check their messages and social media.

EXAMPLE: Technology cannot be used at the dinner table or other eating areas at any time. The main computer in the lounge should be used for doing homework.

4. Privacy

CONSIDERATIONS: Will the parents require access to all email and social media accounts at all times? Will they have the right to perform spot checks? Will they get to know their children's passwords? This is one of the rules that gets the most discussion going at our workshops, as the kids will bemoan that you're 'spying on them' and 'don't trust them'. A fair response is that if they have nothing to hide, they won't mind you checking!

EXAMPLE: Parents may conduct spot checks at any time on any device and will be granted access by the kids providing their current username and password. If the parents discover any activity that contravenes this charter, disciplinary action as outlined in this charter may result.

5. Cyber safety

CONSIDERATIONS: What social networks is your child allowed to have an account on? What other technologies are your child allowed to use (e.g. Skype, Google Hangout)? What settings is your child allowed to have each account set to, and under what circumstances should they allow someone to become their friend/follow them? Note: some networks such as Instagram allow you to control who can and can't follow you and see your posts. Others, such as Twitter, are considered an 'open network' and privacy settings cannot be applied. Don't know enough about social media to feel confident enough to have this discussion? Read the chapter in my book 'No Kidding' on social networking for kids.

EXAMPLE: No one in our family will establish or have access to a social network account until they reach the legal age for use of the network i.e. 13 years old in most cases. Thereafter only an Instagram and Facebook account will be permitted.

6. Content sharing

CONSIDERATIONS: What sort of images can they use on their social network profile? A beach shot in a bikini? Their smiling face in an identifiable school uniform? Or a suitably abstract image with no face at all? What sorts of posts are they allowed to make? Are images of them in underwear or night-time clothing acceptable? What about images in front of the home or school, clearly showing the location? How about their posts? Are swear words acceptable? Is spelling important? Are negative comments or shout-outs about *other people acceptable?*

EXAMPLE: *Where possible we take and post only abstract images that do not identify us or our location, for safety reasons. We definitely do not take or post any provocative images or any images which we may live to regret. We never post profanities, we take care with spelling and we never put people down. We treat others online as we would like to be treated.*

7. Content consumption

CONSIDERATIONS: *What sorts of pages are they permitted to like/follow? What course of action would you like them to take if they don't feel comfortable with something someone is saying or doing online? Notify you? Show you? Will you commit to taking notification seriously and making it a priority to look into it with them? Do you have someone to turn to if the situation is beyond you, such as the account needing to be closed or the police reported to? Note: While rare, there is danger to children from cyber predators. Being flippant about personal information and technology can mean someone knowing exactly where your child is and what they are doing.*

EXAMPLE: **Technology** *should predominantly be used for educational purposes. As a family we agree on a ratio of 80% educational and 20% entertainment purposes. Any contact which feels uncomfortable or confusing will be shared with a parent immediately. All contact by strangers will be shared with a parent regardless.*

8. Consequences of non-compliance with the family charter

CONSIDERATIONS: *If your child won't comply with the mutually agreed charter, what is the consequence? Some families have a 'stepped' discipline programme for example for the first offence—they will lose their technology privileges for one week. Second offence—they lose their technology privileges indefinitely. That means they'll have to use the computers at the public library for homework and go back to the bare bones: the most basic mobile phone without texting capability or internet access. How firm do you want to be, and what does your child think is fair?*

EXAMPLE: A first offence of non-compliance with the charter will result in a one week ban from the use of any technology, except where required for homework. For a second offence the discipline will be loss of the technology for one month, except where required for homework purposes.

And finally, but really importantly, remember the hypocrisy of the old adage 'Do as I say and not as I do'. It wouldn't be fair to set up a one-sided charter and expect it to stick. If you are constantly texting at the dinner table and too distracted for conversations on the couch, the charter will disintegrate into a failed mission. Be prepared to allocate a section to what sort of behaviour your kids can expect of you regarding technology too and potentially what discipline they can take against you! A take-away meal? A foot massage? Make it fun!

Enjoy!

Yvette Adams
www.nokidding.com.au
www.awardshub.com
www.thecreativecollective.com.au
www.thetrainingcollective.com.au

Go to nokidding.com.au/charter to download a free template for your Family Technology Charter, or to access Yvette's book.

SECTION 3

A CHANGE IN THINKING

"Intelligence is the ability to adapt to change"

Mohandas Gandhi

I sat in the plane and stared blankly out of the foggy window, noting glumly that the relentless rain and the grey, damp, drab and foggy envelope surrounding us was a perfect reflection of my mood. I was determinedly, deeply and irrevocably lost in the special and acutely dull despair that is reserved for teenagers in crisis. I was 15 years old, unhappy and stuck winging my way to Abidjan, on the Ivory Coast of West Africa. It felt disastrously wrong. I had been forced from my idyllic home in the Cheshire countryside, literally kicking and screaming, leaving behind my pony, my friends, my freedom and my fledgling adult identity. It seemed to me that my parents had selfishly and heartlessly forced my six brothers, our dog, our cat and me away from all that we knew and into the dark and dismal abyss of the unknown. I was on a stairway to hell and the only way was down.

As a shy child, I spent a great deal of my early years absorbed in my world of animals, my family and my head. As I was skinny and awkward around my peers, for me school had always been a challenge. After struggling through primary school, I was equally uncomfortable and socially inept in high school and totally unprepared to move to the tropics of West Africa. If I could barely get by in Manchester, how on earth was I going to survive in a foreign and unfamiliar place?

The first year was hellish. I was uncomfortable with the climate, the mosquitos, the language, the routine, the school and the food. There are Tumbu flies in Africa that lay their eggs in damp clothes as they hang on the washing line and can burrow under your skin to develop as a large worm-like maggot and hatch. For a 15-year-old girl from the north west of England, whose most challenging creepy-crawly experience prior to Africa had been a bumblebee, this was VERY bad news indeed.

Despite my parents' attempts to cheer me up, I felt extraordinarily out of place and even amongst my large, boisterous and loving family was incredibly lonely. Mistreatment and intimidation continued at my new school from both teachers and students, only this time to add insult to injury it was predominantly in French.

I remember my first day at Bougainville College. It was very hot, the students who were mainly Ivorian, French and Lebanese stared at me curiously.

The teacher introduced me in French, "Here is Karen, our new student. She will be joining us from now on. Is there a spare seat for Karen here?" A girl raised her hand and moved her bag off the seat next to her.

I took a few steps towards her when the teacher said, "By the way, Karen is from England and does not speak any French." As I embarked on that fateful walk towards the back of the classroom, the girl deftly took her bag and placed it back on the chair.

There were a couple of kind souls in my class who would translate all the ugliness during the school breaks so I could at least understand the hostilities that were being thrown my way. My misery continued on for a large part of the first year until we were close to the end of the final term and preparing to take our extended summer holiday, a meaningless distinction in the ever hot and humid West African climate.

Then, one morning, something happened. I suppose you could call it an awakening. As I lay in bed I had a new thought, an interesting thought. What if I could actually be happy regardless of my circumstances? What if it all wasn't quite as bleak as I was imagining it to be? What if the problem wasn't so much my environment but more the story I was telling myself *about* my environment, the way I was looking at things? What if I could find the positives in my world? What if I was missing out on something valuable purely and simply because I wasn't looking in the right place?

> *"Things alter for the worse spontaneously, if they be not altered for the better designedly"*
>
> Francis Bacon

It was a genuine light-bulb moment, a rather major 'ah-ha'. I am quite serious when I say that in that instant *everything* changed. I embraced my previously boring French studies with vigour, looked around for opportunities and paid more attention to the people around me. I refused to return to school as I was now of age and my father offered me a job as a secretary in his office instead. Within three months I was relatively fluent in French. Shortly afterwards I bumped into some school friends who, delighted to know that I could now communicate with them, invited me on a weekend beach trip. In no time I had friends, a job, a firm grasp of a new language and a full and active social life. The ensuing seven years took me to places I previously could never have imagined, to meet people I will never forget and learn skills that I depend on today. In short, I never looked back.

I now consider the painful experiences that I had both as a child in the North of England and in West Africa as some of my greatest gifts, deepest learnings and most precious treasures. Instead of being a burden to me, those challenges have been instrumental in giving me a strong sense of life purpose and are in a large part the drive and motivation for my interest in bullying. Looking back, it is easy for me to identify the thinking that led me to feel intimidated throughout my youth.

I can now see that the 15-year-old Karen was in the *habit* of seeing herself as small and insignificant. She would listen keenly to the comments and jibes of others and place great significance on their actions. She placed her self-confidence, self-worth and her sense of self into the unconscious and unthinking hands of schoolyard peers. In short, she created a habit of giving away her power long before the schoolchildren sought to take it.

The adult version of Karen is under no such illusion. Her sense of self now resides firmly, deeply and steadfastly inside herself. She is interested and willing to hear the opinions and thoughts of others, however she quietly reserves the right to think of herself as she chooses, without apology or shame. She is who she is.

> *"Your opinion of me is none of my business"*
>
> Anonymous

When adversity hits, it often seems that there is no solution. As supposedly the most intelligent life forms on earth, human beings are uniquely skilled at taking themselves into the deepest and darkest pits. We are particularly gifted at turning situations into crises, problems into disasters and difficulties into catastrophes. You only need to watch the evening news to recognise humanity's obsession with all things cataclysmic and our great love of trauma and misfortune. What I was entirely unaware of as a child was my ability to control my thinking, my ability to move from pain to pleasure in an instant and the power that I possessed within me at that time.

Africa was an eye-opener. She provided the perfect environment for me to emerge from my cocoon into the world of adulthood and personal responsibility. She provided a unique opportunity to see myself through very different eyes, to dig deep into my personal resources and to challenge myself and my understanding of the world.

If there is an area in your life that feels limiting, limited, blocked, heavy, stuck or just downright depressing, perhaps there are things you could be doing right now that would change everything, not just for now, but for your lifetime. Perhaps you could do more exercise, take better care of your health and well-being, or become involved in a group where you follow your passion or hobby. Maybe it is time to move house, change jobs or re-evaluate your relationships.

On reflection, is it possible that it is not so much your world as you that is blocked? Before you jump to any conclusion, sit quietly for a moment and consider this: is it in fact possible that the true barrier to your own happiness is actually you?

Perhaps it is time to check out of the pity party and check back in to life. If you are feeling obstructed, helpless, hopeless or alone, now would be a perfect time to move your focus from the problem to the possible solutions. What is there in your environment and in yourself that you can change for the better right this minute? What can you change in the coming weeks and months? What is it that you *can* do to turn things around? What are you missing?

Once you have determined your possible options and solutions, write them down. This will radically improve your chances of bringing them into being. It also helps you stay focused, on track and moving forwards. At all times, whatever you are looking for and whatever you need lies within.

"What lies behind us and what lies before us are tiny matters compared to what lies within us"

Ralph Waldo Emerson

The Old Cracked Pot

A water bearer in India had two large water pots, each hung on the ends of a pole which he carried across his neck. One of the pots was perfectly made and never leaked. The other pot had a crack in it and was only half full by the time the water bearer reached his master's house.

This went on daily, with the bearer delivering only one and a half pots of water to his master's house. The good pot was proud, he was fulfilling the purpose for which he was made; the broken pot was ashamed of his imperfection and his poor accomplishment.

Eventually the cracked pot spoke to the water bearer. "I feel so ashamed of my failure to serve you. I lose half the water I am supposed to deliver because of my leak. Why don't you get a new pot to carry your water?"

"My dear pot," answered the bearer, "I am very happy with what you have delivered to me. Tomorrow, as we go to the stream, pay attention to what you see." The next day the pot looked around on his way to the stream and saw that along one side of the path there were bushes and flowers of all colours but the other side was bare. "I planted the seeds and you watered them for me," explained the bearer, "You have made my walk colourful and entertaining and you have added the pleasure of bringing beautiful flowers to our master's table every day."

Indian Parable

Expressive or Impressive -
Bullies and victims explained

*"The richness of your inner world determines
the quality of your outward experience"*

Merriam Webster Dictionary:
Express - *To force out [press out].*
Impress - *To apply with pressure [press in].*
Energy - *A fundamental element of nature that is transferred between parts
of a system in the production of physical change within the system and usually
regarded as the capacity for doing work.*

Most of us are aware that we can be either energised or drained by the
people we meet. If you walk into a room filled with friends and loved
ones and then move into a room filled with people who have little or no
connection with you, you will feel a difference even if there is no interaction.
We all have our favourite cafés, restaurants, beaches, clubs, and walks that
recharge us, and there are also places that we bypass. There are people we
avoid contact with and there are people we seek out, people who leave us
feeling energised and inspired and people who the mere mention of brings
us down. All this is largely unconscious but demonstrates our understanding
and connection to energy.

Tom Cruise was in fact accurate in the movie *Jerry Maguire* when he
famously said, "You complete me" to Renée Zellweger. Cruise's character of
a money-hungry agent was missing love and connection in his life and she,
as a loving and gentle mother and vulnerable, star struck romantic was the
embodiment of what he lacked. His energy was seeking out the aspect of
himself that was as yet unfulfilled, unrealised and dissatisfied.

The beauty of their story was that the relationship failed as he was hoping
to feel complete simply by being in a relationship and she 'needed' a man
in her life to be happy. They found happiness as a couple only when they
independently took responsibility for their emotional states and were able to

join together as empowered individuals. Both characters eventually learned to complete themselves.

As a means of growth and development, our energy roams around looking for someone who reflects back to us what we most need, not so that they can complete us, but to give us a clearer understanding of what is missing from our experience.

In *Jerry Maguire* the characters are drawn to each other without really understanding why. If instead of jumping into a relationship to bring a sense of wholeness into their lives they worked to understand themselves a little more deeply, they may have had a more enjoyable relationship without spending so much time struggling with each other.

"Every person, all the events of your life are there because you have drawn them there. What you choose to do with them is up to you"

Richard Bach

We pay little attention to the power that lies in our ability to know what and who is good for us and what is not, what we should eat, who we should spend time with, where we should go etc. and yet it is this very ability that leads us to happier, safer and more fulfilled lives. Just as we can see, feel, hear, smell and taste, we can also *sense* or *instinctively register* friendship, kindness, safety, hostility, danger, aggression and deception. It takes time and attention but we are all capable of extending our awareness to each other and our surroundings.

If you are in an abusive and hostile relationship, you will have had plenty of pointers and warnings along the way. These pointers come in the forms of physical, emotional and sensory cues and are available to each of us at all times.

The human race appears to be singularly adept at avoidance strategies. We are able to ignore cues about our health and well-being to a spectacular and often catastrophic degree. We use compulsions and desires to guide our behaviours, resulting in an almost obsessive attachment to television, gossip, celebrity, success, work, sport and any number of distractive behaviours which cause us to not attend to our lives either in a physical or practical sense, or indeed in an emotional or psychological sense. We are simply not paying attention to the fundamentals.

"Human beings, who are almost unique in having the ability to learn from the experience of others, are also remarkable for their apparent disinclination to do so"

Douglas Adams

Our inability to notice these cues comes from a lack of awareness as well as the desensitising effects of processed foods, technology, media, alcohol, illicit and legal drugs, and environmental toxins. Drug and alcohol abuse and the insensitivity and unconsciousness that accompany our behaviours pale into insignificance compared to the everyday methods we employ to become numb to our lives. An average working Joe or elite executive can be as disconnected from themselves as a chronic drug abuser. We use different methods and our lives appear very different on the surface; however, we manage to produce the same result.

Through the expressive/impressive energy model my hope is to induce healthy discussion which in turn will help develop new practical solutions to modern bullying problems. Obviously a fresh approach is called for as conventional wisdom has not as yet delivered effective answers. If it had, bullying would no longer be a problem in our world and ergo, there would be no need for this book.

In using the term expressive and impressive energy I put forward a theoretical understanding of bullying and how it comes into being. Here we will delve into the unseen world of energy exchange and transfer, as it has been described through scientific investigation and as it is experienced by us in some form or another.

> *"No problem can be solved from the same level of consciousness that created it"*
>
> Albert Einstein

Science has discovered that electromagnetic energy is exchanged when two living beings come into contact with each other. This energy is subtle and invisible, however it is ever present. Human beings are in fact walking, talking energy transmitters. For us to understand bullying in full, we will need to explore this energy exchange.

On one hand we are talking about energy in a practical, logical and analytical fashion and on the other hand we are talking about the nebulous world of gut instinct and intuition and how this applies to the relationship between bully and victim.

The expressive/impressive model has a resonance with Swiss psychiatrist and psychotherapist Carl Jung's extrovert/introvert principles, which also form a prominent part of the Myers-Briggs Type Indicator. In principle it is an elaboration or extension of the extrovert/introvert theory into the realms of energy exchange and intuition.

The words extrovert and introvert are *popularly* understood to mean sociable or outgoing and shy and withdrawn. These are not accurate representations of the extrovert/introvert model, as extroverts can be extremely shy and introverts sociable and outgoing. Extroversion in its true sense is better explained as gaining energy through action and interaction.

> *"The state of your life is nothing more than a reflection of your state of mind"*
>
> Dr. Wayne W. Dyer

Introversion is better understood as gaining energy through reflection and solitude. The expressive/impressive model illustrates how extrovert and introvert behaviours manifest in the bully/victim cycle.

Expressive/impressive energy at work

The study of bio-electromagnetics has been able to scientifically measure the interaction between electromagnetic fields and biological entities. It is now widely understood that every human being on this planet has a unique and noticeable energy field that permeates and is emitted from their body. This energy is recognised by each of us both physically and subtly and forms a key element in the bully/victim experience. In times past it was known as intuition.

In many cultures an understanding of the energetic or unseen relationship between sentient beings has been passed down through the generations using ritual, tradition and word of mouth. Partly due to our increasing desensitisation to our natural environment, many of these practices have been abandoned by Western culture or are maintained in an obscure and cursory fashion within our religious or spiritual practices. As with any of our physical attributes, if we fail to consciously employ our intuition, over time we lose the ability to do so.

We have built into our biochemistry, tangible and measurable ways of sensing and relating to each other that do not depend on any form of conscious communication. This is a powerful and valuable tool which is often given little or no value in our current cultural story. A rudimentary way to test your electromagnetic field is to close your eyes and have a friend silently approach you from behind. Notice when you can actually feel their presence. Another way is to place your hand opposite a friend's and notice that you can sense or feel their energy before your hands touch.

Imagine each of us as simply a ball of energy and the expressive energy is unconsciously searching for an energetic match in the impressive energy in order to feel balanced or whole. A person with impressive energy *attracts* expressive energy to energetically match their state, like two pieces of a jigsaw fitting together.

If the two energy types have healthy boundaries, confidence and self-esteem, this can be a fortuitous and beneficial experience. If however they have poor boundaries, confidence and self-esteem the relationship will inevitably be fraught.

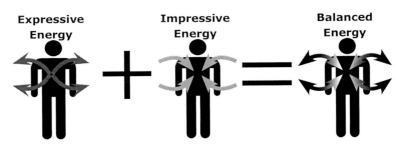

Expressive Energy + Impressive Energy = Balanced Energy

We are attracted to our energetic match so if we ourselves are out of balance, our energetic match will be also. In unhealthy relationships we tend to be attracted to our opposite energy which plays out in an unhealthy and potentially harmful way. In order to resolve feelings of incompleteness we seek out a partner who complements and matches our imbalance. The partner will have an equal amount of issues to redress in themselves and potentially push both parties into an uncomfortable co-dependent relationship.

In bully/victim relationships you will find that commonly an extremely expressive energy and an extremely impressive energy type will attract each other. This can manifest in schools as the archetypal jock versus nerd scenario and in relationships as an abusive and dominant spouse with an overly passive and submissive partner. Each person attracts and experiences the balance they are lacking in themselves.

"To bring anything into your life, imagine that it's already there"

Richard Bach

As with all interpretations of human behaviour, none of us falls exclusively into one specific behaviour type and we all possess elements of each; however, there are some people who sit in extremes in either one or the other. Neither expressive nor impressive are more desirable as attributes as both personality types have their advantages and disadvantages and bring colour and richness to the human experience.

It is important to note that bullies and victims can be either expressive or impressive personality types. Expressive does not mean bully and impressive does not mean victim, as the power in the relationship can lie in the hands of either.

There are many circumstances where the impressive personality type holds the balance of power and bullies the expressive personality type. An impressive personality may employ ruse and subterfuge to control and dominate the relationship. They may withhold affection, be aloof, absent and unconscious of the needs of others. They can also be neglectful, self-absorbed at times, or play dumb to avoid confrontation. This is the most common form of playground bullying where gossip, ostracising, cyber bullying and social isolation play a big part in the bully/victim dynamic.

If the expressive personality type dominates the relationship they are inclined to be over-zealous, overtly pushy, demanding, intimidating and lacking in emotional control. An expressive person could also use physical force. Both expressive and impressive personality types are capable of displaying all of these behaviours as they are not necessarily exclusively the domain of one or the other.

"No one heals himself by wounding another"

St Ambrose

Characteristics of expressive and impressive energy types

Expressive energy characteristics

Expressive Energy

- Outwardly confident
- High energy
- Action orientated and active
- Enjoys the attention of others
- Often extrovert
- Gregarious
- Enthusiastic
- Dislikes being alone
- Interested in the external world
- Enjoys groups of friends
- Likes team sports and group activities
- Requires physical stimulation
- Is unhindered by noise
- Likes physically creative tasks and manual work
- Is uncomfortable or bored with stillness
- Spends little time checking in with their feelings
- Is often perceived as a bully although this is not always the case.

Negative attributes: Anger, frustration, jealousy, insecurity, dominance
Positive attributes: Enthusiasm, creativity, zest for life, action

Impressive energy characteristics

Impressive Energy

- ❈ Lacking outward confidence
- ❈ Can have low energy
- ❈ Reserved and reflective
- ❈ Interested in their inner world
- ❈ Calm
- ❈ Dislikes attention
- ❈ Has a few close friends
- ❈ Prefers 1:1 or small groups or being alone
- ❈ Often introvert
- ❈ Observant
- ❈ Dislikes team sports and large group activities
- ❈ Requires mental stimulation
- ❈ Prefers intellectual or artistic tasks
- ❈ Checks in with their feelings before making plans or decisions
- ❈ Is uncomfortable with noise
- ❈ Is often perceived as the victim although this is not always the case.

Negative attributes: Fear, sadness, apathy, victim mentality, anxiety

Positive attributes: Kindness, gentleness, awareness, creativity, empathy

We are perfectly able to manage when and how we distribute our energy and to whom we give it. There are no circumstances in which you can be *forced* to take on the energy of another regardless of physical proximity. Both Mahatma Gandhi through his life's work and Victor Frankl in his book *Man's Search for Meaning* (see page 105) demonstrate that the human spirit cannot be affected by external conditions unless they choose it to be so. Becoming conscious of energy is one way to take control of your inner world and cease to be at the mercy of your physical experience. This is equally true for people who have suffered great physical or emotional trauma.

Ideally the expressive personality type and the impressive personality type will ultimately recognise their imbalance and strive to cultivate the aspect of themselves that requires growth and development. Identifying strengths and weaknesses allows us the opportunity to become self-aware. When facing abuse and bullying we gain from understanding where the problem lies and what aspects of ourselves require energising or minimising in order to achieve balance.

Understanding your own energy patterns can be a light-bulb moment for many people. It can explain so much about your relationships and why some work and others cause stress and upset. It can also be a key to unlocking the door to a healthier, happier and more creative environment for yourself.

*"I will not let anyone walk through my mind
with their dirty feet"*

Mahatma Gandhi

Boundaries and Positive Self Talk

"Very little is needed to make a happy life;
it is all within yourself, in your way of thinking"

Marcus Aurelius Antoninus

Your happiness is determined by your self-talk. If you are unhappy, your self-talk will tend to be negative and you will not be creating, growing or developing to your full potential. Creativity, growth and development lie on the outside edge of your comfort zone. Your comfort zone is determined by your boundaries. If you are being bullied and picked on and find yourself in pain, your boundaries may be too low or too high. To remedy this you will need to pay attention to both your boundaries and your self-talk. Some physical situations are indeed impossible to change, such as incarceration or physical limitations and yet your state of mind, degree of happiness and attitude are always determined by you.

Completely immobilised, wheelchair-bound and unable to talk, Stephen Hawking has made a gargantuan contribution to the scientific world. However he has also brought to the world at large a radical and evolutionary idea. He has proven to us that happiness and creative ability do not remotely depend on physical capacity and are entirely a result of our own thinking. This demonstration of extraordinary power and ingenuity gives pause for thought as he is a living breathing example of humanity's ability to find not only joy and purpose in seemingly dire circumstances but to make an enormous contribution along the way.

"Although I cannot move and I have to speak through a computer, in my mind I am free"

Stephen Hawking

Stephen Hawking's achievements may on the surface seem rather intimidating and out of reach for those of us experiencing difficulties with self-esteem and confidence, but the system he applies to overcome his challenges is the same for all of us. In order to find peace and fulfilment within yourself, you need a strategy. This strategy can be applied in the face of bullies just as it can be applied when dealing with catastrophe, trauma or tragedy.

We tend to respond to bullies in one of two ways, through a pain pattern, which keeps us stuck in the problem and leads to ongoing and limiting experiences, or a gain pattern, which allows us to move forward, learn, grow and evolve out of the problem.

For example, if someone were to make hurtful comments about your body, you could respond in a variety of ways:

Pain Pattern:

1. Believe the bully—negative self-talk
2. Remove yourself from the situation but continue to believe the bully—negative self-talk
3. Withdraw into your inner world and continue to believe the bully—negative self-talk.

Gain Pattern:

1. Ignore the bully and believe in yourself—positive self-talk
2. Change the situation and believe in yourself—positive-self-talk
3. Withdraw into your inner world with positive self-talk.

The third option in each list, withdrawing, is often only chosen when the other options have been exhausted. Withdrawal is often used in situations of severe abuse, trauma, drug and alcohol addiction or incarceration. A great deal of mental anguish, memory loss and potential mental illness is as a result of withdrawing with negative self-talk. People who withdraw with positive self-talk are far more likely to experience positive outcomes from their situation, regardless of the pain and trauma involved.

Viktor Frankl commenting in his book *Man's Search for Meaning* on his experiences as a prisoner in Nazi concentration camps during the Holocaust:

> *"I understood how a man who has nothing left in this world still may know bliss, be it only for a brief moment, in the contemplation of his beloved. In a position of utter desolation, when man cannot express himself in positive action, when his only achievement may consist in enduring his sufferings in the right way—an honourable way—in such a position man can, through loving contemplation of the image he carries of his beloved, achieve fulfilment."*

His words show us the unbelievable potential of the human spirit to overcome even the most torturous of experiences with love and a strong and rich connection to our inner world. Our life looks and sounds the way it does to us because of the *choices* made by each one of us. Nobody chooses your story for you, nobody chooses your interpretation and nobody creates your path.

Ultimately the decision of how willing you are to allow that person to operate in your space and what behaviours are acceptable depends greatly on your own vision of the world and your ability to set up *non-negotiable* boundaries. Therein lies the real answer to the bully/victim cycle. Self-confidence, a willingness to take action and the ability to be clear about personal boundaries is a powerful formula for healing and/or ending toxic relationships.

"One's dignity may be assaulted, vandalised and cruelly mocked, but it can never be taken away unless it is surrendered"

Michael J. Fox

The Power Within - *Alison's Story*

"You make the road by walking on it"

Nicaraguan saying

In 2008, Alison co-founded the company Photoshow on DVD, specialising in multimedia, slideshows and video production for families and businesses. Her mission is to help people honour life by celebrating and recognising their achievements, through photographic and video memories.

Alison shares her poignant and personal story which speaks of triumph in the face of great personal pain. She is a keen campaigner on the journey to overcome bullying and is writing a book of memoirs.

My memories of childhood are ones of turbulence and dread. In my first 16 years of life, I developed many fears and phobias and at 14 years old, I contemplated suicide.

For years I suffered in silence, feeling helpless and worthless, always withdrawn and very quiet. I was always alone, felt awkward and couldn't fit in. I was 16 years old when I started working full time to support myself and at times working extra jobs just to survive. I was very lonely and my path was often filled with darkness.

I was of Portuguese heritage and born in Singapore, where status is so important. If you came from a broken family, you were a black sheep or a failure.

It was during this time I searched to find meaning in my life. I now strongly believe that when you experience failure, you will always be presented with an opportunity to learn a valuable lesson. What you do with this lesson is entirely up to you, in the choices you make. Our mindset and attitude becomes crucial for growth. Everyone designs their own life.

Eventually my mother and I realised we had to leave. With only $600 in our bank account and the clothes on our backs, Mum and

I started our journey to renew our broken life. It was a very dark and hard road, but it has led us to an extraordinary life.

Instead of holding on to my past I chose forgiveness. Moving into a place of forgiveness gave me a powerful release of energy and helped me to find peace. It led me to the renewal of my life and ended the sadness, hatred, regret and depression. Forgiveness opened my heart to compassion and love. I finally felt free and was able to move on with my life.

By changing my mindset and believing in myself, I worked my way from a bank cashier right through to corporate and was given the opportunity to travel the world. I volunteered to help kids from non-English speaking families and broken homes. They could not afford a tutor so I taught them English and maths. I have lived my dreams, met my wonderful husband and have been blessed with two wonderfully kind and creative children.

Growth first begins within your mindset and positive attitude toward life. Mum taught me very early to believe in the impossible. When I took action, the Universe or God assisted me all the way. I have seen many unexplained situations that I call miracles and this has strengthened my beliefs. I have taken leaps of faith which when I look back seem truly unbelievable, yet all it took was to feel worthy and trust my instincts.

Recently, my seven-year-old son was teased and bullied at school. I panicked because I did not want him to feel what I felt as a child. My good friend Karen reminded me that we need to look within ourselves to discover our strength. I felt empowered to help my son draw upon his own strength and he did. He has that survival instinct within him; all he needed was to know that I would always be there, ever ready to support him.

He is a very quiet, gentle, intelligent kid who is always happy. When asked what he would like to be as a grown up, his answer was, "To be happy as a normal parent, like my mum and dad. I would love to have my own kids too". For me to be able to pass this on to my son at such a young age, is truly creating a new path for future generations.

As a result of my past, my difficulties, my trials and my tribulations, I have learnt a very important lesson. For me, simplicity is the key to happiness.

Alison Laverty
www.photoshowondvd.com.au

The Misfits, the Fidgets, the Waywards and the Mischievous

"I'm not going to buy my kids an encyclopaedia.
Let them walk to school like I did"

Yogi Berra

There is a percentage of children who are bullied at school who also struggle with school work and socialising. Some of these children have been flagged by the school or child specialists as having ADHD or other related disorders, and some are students who find the classroom or learning environment challenging and lose confidence and focus as a result.

ADHD is characterised by inattentiveness, difficulty listening and following instructions, lack of organisation and inability to complete tasks, difficulty socialising and playing with others, excessive fidgeting, dislike of tasks requiring mental effort, difficulty controlling behaviour and hyperactivity. To a degree, these traits also appear in other children who are not coping with the school environment.

Statistically, children with ADHD more easily find themselves caught in a cycle of bullying as a result of the difficulties they have socialising and fitting in at school. Some studies put the percentage of ADHD sufferers involved in school bullying both as victim and bully as high as 58%.

Differences in learning styles have profound implications on the classroom experience. Neil Flemming's VARK model identifies four major learning preferences found in students:

1. Visual—seeing and thinking in pictures
2. Auditory—listening
3. Read/write—the modality of words
4. Kinaesthetic/tactile—active or physical exploration of the world

The use of this model in instruction allows teachers to prepare classes that address the varied learning styles of their students. Students can also use the model to improve their educational experience by focusing on what benefits them the most.

Our current education system favours auditory and read/write learning styles, while often disenfranchising the visual and kinaesthetic learners. As a result some students swan through tests and assessments and others freeze with fear at the thought. Some listen to the lesson and need very little revision and others struggle to follow the conversation at all.

Fidgeting, squirming and being easily distracted are considered inappropriate in children and many are being diagnosed and medicated as a consequence. Medicating children in order to integrate them into an education system as opposed to adapting or modifying the system is one of the biggest social catastrophes of our time. Some of these children drop out or leave school with self-esteem at a low ebb. The failure and dropout rate could well have less to do with ability and intelligence and more to do with neurological wiring.

Teachers alone are not to be blamed for the difficulties some students have in the classroom and most do their very best to support pupils in their care. The demands to hit targets and standards are manifold and there is no time to develop specialised programmes to engage, distract or connect to each and every student. There are however schools that have good overall success rates and a deep interest in the confidence, esteem and well-being of their students. These schools inevitably have strong compassionate leaders who possess vision, passion and purpose.

Bullying can only flourish where confidence and self-esteem is low, ergo children who are finding it difficult to cope with not only the social and emotional pressure of peers but also with a sense of anxiety about their academic ability are inevitably at risk.

> *"Many highly talented, brilliant, creative people think they're not—because the thing they were good at school wasn't valued, or was actually stigmatised"*
>
> Ken Robinson

> *"Motivation and self-esteem are crucial factors in raising standards of achievement. All young people tend to be considered as able or less able in education, primarily on the basis of academic performance. But many of these less able children may have significant abilities in areas which are overlooked by schools. This can be a powerful source of disaffection and under-achievement"*
>
> Sir Ken Robinson

40 years ago, when my husband Wayne was at primary school his mother received a call from the teacher asking if she could kindly walk him around the block several times before bringing him to school as he had too much energy and was disruptive in class. Evidently, in the 1970s some schools clearly acknowledged the need to express and dissipate energy, and equally understood the link between repressed energy and our ability to learn.

Wayne's personality and temperament lean strongly towards expressive and extrovert behaviour. This thankfully un-medicated overactive child put his energy into a sporting career throughout school and high school, and learned guitar. His boundless energy has led him to create a successful career in management and customer service. For him, nothing much has changed since his primary school experience. His walk around the block has become a surf, a workout, a run or a new personal or business challenge. He still needs to constantly channel his boundless energy into a pursuit of some sort, very rarely sits still and can do a marvellous guitar performance of 'Suspicious Minds'.

Like many children, it was in Wayne's nature to constantly be on the move. Schools need effective strategies for dealing with high energy children so they do not go through the education system feeling like misfits, failures or hopeless cases. The future can be bright for energetic and enthusiastic people, we just need to help them through school…

"The only thing that interferes with my learning is my education"

Albert Einstein

How to Artfully Avoid Fitting In

"Let's face it. No kid in high school feels as though they fit in"

Stephen King

So where's the value in avoiding 'fitting in?' As we each live in a world constructed in our heads, our sense of fitting or not fitting in is also a construction. The absolute truth of the matter is none of us fit in, which paradoxically means all of us fit in as misfits. To attempt to fit in is futile. If in the unlikely instance you did in fact achieve a sense of belonging, you would then be beleaguered with the constant fear of losing that which you belong to.

There is really no need to fear. Your sense of not fitting in actually connects you to all other beings on the planet. At a deep and fundamental level we all belong, we are all kin and we are all connected, however at a superficial, physical level we are exquisitely unique and will *never* meet someone who is *exactly* like us.

If we drop the favourite myth of the ego which is that we have to belong to a group entity, we become free to be ourselves: unique, quirky, interesting, dull, light-hearted, morose, unreasonable, incongruous and perfectly imperfect.

If you are determined to fit in to something, do so by not fitting in. Join the group of people who are choosing to no longer focus on pleasing others but following what is right and good in their own hearts. There is no group, there is no 'them' and there are no 'others'. Every group you identify will have differences and conflicts. Every family you meet will have their challenges. Every team you join will have their difficulties and hurdles to overcome, and every school you go to will have a full and varied repertoire of personality types, behaviours, temperaments, hostilities and degrees of kindness.

"We have nothing to fear but fear itself... and, of course, the boogieman"

Pat Paulsen

You will never have a lasting or permanent feeling of fitting in, but if you choose to still yourself and focus inwards you will find a deep sense of connectedness and belonging that can never ever be taken from you. Your strength, your sense of community, your connection and your power, right this minute lies within.

The Power of the Victim

"If your happiness depends on what somebody else does,
I guess you do have a problem"

Richard Bach

In any bullying situation, absolute power lies with the victim. If there is no victim, the bully can't bully. If there is no one available for the bully to vent their aggression, hostility and pain upon, there is absolutely nothing they can do about it.

Human beings on the whole are loath to change behaviour unless absolutely necessary. Many people wait for a health scare before they make changes to their diet or exercise regimes. Others endure unhappy or painful relationships where both the perpetrator and the victim are miserable and yet many marriages have gone a lifetime in this pattern. If you are waiting for the bully to take the first step then you may well be waiting in vain.

In general, a bully will remain comfortable with the status quo as the predicament poses less of a problem for them than for you. The evolution of the problem almost entirely depends on the victim either removing themselves from the situation or creating a significant shift in the relationship and the balance of power. Only then will the bully experience the necessary sense of loss that could motivate them into making important changes to their behaviour. To remove yourself from the role of victim is the kindest act of all. To step away from a bully is an act of love.

The victim is also capable of leading a happy and fulfilled life if they understand how to abandon their insecurities, move back into their own personal power, establish good boundaries and be vigilant and conscious of the behaviours of others.

"You are not here merely to make a living. You are here to enable the world to live more amply, with greater vision, and with a finer spirit of hope and achievement. You are here to enrich the world. You impoverish yourself if you forget this errand"

Woodrow Wilson

Creating Confidence

"Go within or go without"

Neale Donald Walsch

Oxford Dictionary:

Confident - 1. *Feeling or showing confidence in oneself or one's abilities or qualities, e.g. 'she was a confident, outgoing girl'.*

2. Feeling or showing certainty about something, e.g. 'this time they're confident of a happy ending'.

There are two distinct forms of confidence, *outward* confidence and *inner* confidence, which have different connotations and engender different results. Confidence is described as feeling or showing confidence, *feeling* being inner confidence and *showing* being outward confidence. Here perhaps we have another pointer towards the *expressive* and *impressive* use of energy and how it manifests in human experience.

Outward Confidence

Outward confidence, stemming from a place of connection, enthusiasm, creativity and joy, is a pleasure to behold and intoxicating to the spirit. Outward confidence should be supported, celebrated and encouraged. When our outward expression matches our innermost desires we can truly say we have found deep contentment and happiness. Outward confidence, when stemming from a firmly entrenched inner confidence, is deliciously contagious. This attribute is not solely the domain of the rich and famous and can be found in people from all walks of life.

"Health is the greatest possession. Contentment is the greatest treasure. Confidence is the greatest friend. Non-being is the greatest joy"

Lao Tzu

Children who possess a strong sense of inner and outward confidence can come across as impertinent or cheeky to adults who do not possess the same qualities. Being innately curious creatures, when someone exudes both inner and outward confidence we find ourselves drawn, as if by magnetic force, to investigate and discover what it is exactly that they have to share.

"Look, I really don't want to wax philosophic, but I will say that if you're alive, you've got to flap your arms and legs, you've got to jump around a lot, you've got to make a lot of noise, because life is the very opposite of death"

Mel Brooks

Outward confidence is not to be confused with showmanship or flamboyance. Outward confidence which is created as a display to detract attention from a person's hidden insecurities is one of the primary drivers for bullying.

The showman strategy can be used as a means to disguise insecurity or self-consciousness. The person becomes a performer and develops attention-seeking behaviour to distract attention from their insecurity. This is demonstrated in the classroom as trouble-making, bullying or clownish behaviour. Of course clowning around, misbehaving and having fun is not purely the domain of insecure and self-conscious people. There are many clowns in the world who do so for the pure joy of it as a result of an irrepressible spirit.

Outwardly displayed confidence, when stemming from insecurity and lack, can be a huge liability. It is akin to walking into an exam with bluster, swagger, charm and confidence without having previously studied. Regardless of the performance, they would still fail the exam.

Disguising awkwardness with displays of outward flamboyance can only serve temporarily as a cover or shield. It can attract short-term followers or supporters but is nigh on impossible to sustain and eventually the façade crumbles.

This personality attribute can show in a variety of ways:

- Friends who give and withdraw friendship, running power plays to test out their ability to influence others.
- A person who acts as the life and soul of the party, gregarious and outgoing, however is harbouring deep insecurities, jealousy and bitterness.
- People who wear a mask of friendship, friendliness and confidence. When faced with exposure they move on to new territory, new friendships and remain entrenched in the same pattern, failing to address their issues or insecurities.

Some artistic, theatrical and musical entertainers use performance as an outlet for introverted behaviours or to distract them from deep insecurities. Creative expression can be healing, calming and balancing for people who do not possess a naturally outgoing personality or who experience overwhelming negative emotions due to personal circumstances.

"Enemies are so stimulating"

Katharine Hepburn

Feelings of insecurity are not necessarily *bad* per se. Much of our music, theatre, art, books and films have been produced by people who suffer from very low confidence and self-esteem. Some of the best music around has been written as a result of depression, anguish and loss. The 60s music scene was driven by the need to resist and revolt against unresponsive governments, oppressive systems and restrictive social policies.

In a world steeped in corporate and political trickery, misinformation and subterfuge, the creative power of humanity is not to be underestimated. Significant difficulties and challenge can provide hidden opportunities. Some of us find that we have untapped creativity and unrealised potential as a *result* of our suffering and not in spite of it.

There are very few people in the world who can truly attest to being at peace with themselves. The rest of us are left to muddle along as best we can. Finding positive avenues for creative expression is a huge step in the right direction. If you have a child who lacks confidence, encourage them to participate in a musical, theatrical or artistic pursuit of some sort. Becoming skilled in any artistic endeavour regardless of whether it becomes a lifetime passion or not, will always serve to provide the voiceless and discounted an opportunity to shine.

"Politicians may well have our heads but musicians will always have our hearts"

Expression, like confidence, comes in different forms and can as easily be ascribed to writing a private journal as it can be to performing on a stage. What we do know is that if you can overcome the fear of expressing yourself you will have come a step further along on the journey to confidence and self-esteem and are less likely to be immobilised by the fear of what other people think.

Expression is fundamental to all living creatures and is how we make change, manifest creatively and evolve. We all possess a strong and instinctive desire to experience ourselves as valuable and valued, which drives us to seek opportunities for creation and self-expression. We wish to be noticed, we wish to be appreciated and we wish very much to be loved. If this inbuilt and intrinsic desire to create is left unfulfilled it drives us to compulsive and sometimes destructive behaviours, or despondency and depression. We are most comfortable when we are free to express ourselves without censure or ridicule. We experience a great deal of personal satisfaction and deep sense of happiness when we are able to excel in some form or another through creative, practical or intellectual achievement.

Inner Confidence

Inner confidence has a completely different feel to it and is the basis and essential counterpart of true outward confidence. Inner confidence is a sense of certainty or purpose. It does not feel the need to justify or soap-box its belief system. Inner confidence stems from unwavering *personal* truths about life, and living. It comes from a connection and understanding of self and the expression of gifts and talents. Inner confidence is individual and unique, un-teachable and unlearn-able. Each person discovers their own inner confidence in their own time and in their own way. Just as all humanity differs subtly, so each person's inner landscape is unique and unfathomable. Many of us spend a lifetime seeking this sense of confidence, direction and certainty. Some children however, are born with a certainty of purpose that is astonishing.

> *"Thousands of candles can be lit from a single candle, and the life of the candle will not be shortened. Happiness never decreases by being shared"*
>
> Buddha

The key word here is *certainty*. There is no doubt that we live in an uncertain world which delivers choices and opportunities as equally as it delivers challenges. No two people experience the same opportunities or the same challenges, so no one else can possibly see the potential that exists inside you or how you are to achieve your goals.

> *"A woman is like a tea bag – you can't tell how strong she is until you put her in hot water"*
>
> Eleanor Roosevelt

There is great value in finding your own sense of direction, focus and purpose. With a sense of purpose comes certainty. It is our sense of certainty that helps us move towards our goals and dreams.

If you possess a strong connection and understanding of self you are more likely to be able to say what you need to say and do what you need to do with or without an audience. When you are connected to your purpose and know who you are, you are able to take situations more lightly. Speaking to a crowd, performing on stage, competing in a race or sports event, taking an exam, being bullied or put down and any number of other potentially stressful situations actually become less daunting and less noticeable as problems.

The person in possession of inner confidence will find it easy to switch between both aspects of themselves, the performer or expressive self and the witness/observer, impressive self, and is equally comfortable in either role.

A person who lacks a strong connection to self, a strong sense of who they are, will either be inclined to perform continuously to maintain the charade and prevent people from discovering their insecurities, or withdraw deeply into themselves for fear of being discovered. Both these methods can lead to a deep sense of unease, anxiety and discomfort.

If you wish to explore, energise or activate your connection to your inner confidence and intuition try some of the suggestions in the tools and techniques section or refer to the recommended reading list at the back of the book.

"The only thing that is constant is change"

Heraclitus

Horse Sense - *Tanja's Story*

"If you paint in your mind a picture of bright and happy expectations, you put yourself into a condition conducive to your goal"

Norman Vincent Peale

Tanja Mitton, a world-leading Equestrian Mindset Coach and author of *Seven Steps to the Mindset of an Equestrian Champion* uses confidence and self-esteem techniques to assist horse riders, from anxious and nervous beginner riders up to elite-level competitors. Through these techniques she has witnessed profoundly transformational results in her clients and interestingly, in their horses.

Whether you ride horses or not, you will find in this story a powerful demonstration of how deeply our inner landscape affects our external experience and how simple it can be to bring about conclusive and lasting change.

Have you ever lost your confidence and wondered how to get it back?

I find that horses provide us the greatest feedback on how we feel about ourselves as well as the people and animals around us.

Horses are flight animals, meaning they are very intuitive and sensitive to their environment. They are able to pick up on the slightest change in energy and respond according to their instincts. A horse in survival mode runs away from danger until it feels safe enough to stop again.

One of the most common fears of riders is the fear of losing control. This can be the fear of losing control of the horse's speed, the horse itself or losing control of the situation.

Sue came to me a couple of years ago and told me she had massive problems with her horse. It began with her feeling unsafe when riding by herself and gradually developed into riding in general. When she rang me she was in tears and told me she was thinking of selling her horse and giving up riding.

When I met with Sue as part of a clinic, she told me she might not be able to bring her horse to the riding club due to difficulties catching it and then putting it on the float. She was so emotional when she told me about all the problems she was having that even I could feel a change in her energy as she became more wound up and stressed.

Sue said that she planned to get up at 5am the next day (the clinic started at 8am) to allow her an hour to catch the horse. She figured she would still have another hour to load her horse (normally loading a horse on a float takes ten minutes) and then she was hoping to make it in time for the start of the clinic.

I sat down with Sue and asked her how she knew the horse would be difficult to catch. Her reply was that the horse knew when she wanted to go somewhere, a clinic or a lesson, and that's when he wouldn't be caught.

I told her that in my experience horses are very smart but not that smart! Horses don't know when a lesson is coming up and they don't have a rational, language-based brain to think about how to annoy the rider. They react purely to their environment and what they instinctively pick up.

When we talked further, I learned that Sue had some difficult lessons in the past where she came away believing she wasn't good enough as a rider. Some of the other riding club members had said she might be too old to ride and that she was better off selling the horse to let a younger, more experienced rider take over.

With time, this produced a lot of stress for Sue and she started to lose confidence in herself and her abilities. This is something I see often in any area of life, not just in the horse world. People are being told they can't do something or they shouldn't do something and they translate it into:

- ❋ *I am not good enough*
- ❋ *I am not worthy enough*
- ❋ *I don't deserve it*
- ❋ *Everything I do is wrong.*

I asked Sue to write a list of ten things she did well and was proud of herself for. She looked at me with a blank expression and really struggled to put pen to paper.

After a while she managed to write out ten achievements, then cried as she read them out to me. We talked about how much she had already achieved and how many things she did well with her horse. Next I asked her to tell me what would normally go through her mind on the morning of a lesson or clinic. She told me she would think about all the people who would be at the clinic and how everyone was so much better than her.

She would imagine what the instructor would ask her to do and how she would deal with it, particularly how she would get it wrong. It was very clear that all her focus was on the belief that she wasn't good enough and that she would fail.

We went back to her achievements list and started to talk about how she could use all the things she had written down to become more positive about her lessons. We spoke about the options available to her if she was asked to do something that she didn't know how to do. A simple response could be to ask the instructor for help.

We also looked at the people who made her feel most uncomfortable and spoke about how to establish some personal boundaries.

I stayed at Sue's house that night and asked her to set her alarm for 6.30am the next day instead of 5am. I also asked her to make herself a cup of tea before she went outside to catch the horse and to give herself time to think about all the things she had on her achievement list, and how much fun the clinic was going to be.

The next morning Sue knocked on my door at 6am with a big smile. She didn't quite trust herself so she got up at 5.30am then made herself a cup of tea and did exactly what we talked about. When she went outside she found her horse standing at the gate of his paddock waiting for her. She put the halter on and he came out and walked straight onto the float for her without any hesitation. In fact she had to take him off the float again as it was far too early to go!

Sue's focus had changed and the way she spoke to herself that morning was different to her usual self talk. The energy she gave out drew the horse towards her instead of making him run away. The horse always wanted to be there for her, she just didn't realise that with her self-destructive thoughts she had driven him away.

The clinic went very well and both Sue and her horse did an amazing job. Sue rang me a couple of months later and told me she had taken on board what we talked about, not just in her horse riding but also at work and with her family.

She said her husband and kids had commented on how calm and happy she was and at work she had learned to say no and establish her boundaries.

From that day on, whenever her horse would run away to avoid being caught, she would go into the kitchen, make herself a cup of tea and sit down to go through her achievement list until she felt calm and happy again.

After that she would always find the horse waiting by the gate.

Tanja Mitton
Equestrian Mindset Coach
www.equestriansuccessmindset.com

The X Factor

"Nothing in this world can take the place of persistence. Talent will not: nothing is more common than unsuccessful men with talent. Genius will not: unrewarded genius is almost a proverb. Education will not: the world is full of educated derelicts. Persistence and determination alone are omnipotent"

Calvin Coolidge

There is a powerful link between bullying, assumed victimisation and low self-worth. It is clear that when our confidence and self-esteem depend on external forces, we are at the mercy of our environment and as such dependent on the behaviour of others for our happiness. So, how do you improve confidence and self-esteem in either yourself or your children? The answer lies partly in a deeper understanding of the elusive X factor.

The X factor is generally thought to be a consequence of fame, success or accomplishment as opposed to being the cause. The reason why it has been named the X factor is because it is difficult to describe or understand and consequently difficult to reproduce.

On the journey to finding the X factor it is necessary to focus less on creating confidence and self-esteem and more on the actual process of learning to trust your instincts and developing self-belief. Confidence and self-esteem are by-products of a shift we make deep inside ourselves. The X factor is an energetic process that is triggered when you connect to your purpose and your gifts.

"The quieter you become, the more you can hear"

Ram Das

Our Western culture with its male dominated, analytical and logical approach to life and evolution has caused us to lose touch with our ability to intuit situations or to use our feelings as a *practical and accepted* tool for well-being and decision making. Instead of being encouraged to embrace and examine our feelings, we have been shamed into minimising and ignoring much of what we innately know to be true. We have also been minimising and ignoring the truth of who we are and our purpose here on the planet.

> *"If you are neutral in situations of injustice, you have chosen the side of the oppressor. If an elephant has its foot on the tail of a mouse, and you say that you are neutral, the mouse will not appreciate your neutrality"*
>
> Desmond Tutu

This anomaly has been caused by a combination of many factors. Many of us are living with little or no relationship to our natural environment; we are no longer instructed in the stories and traditions of our ancestors and have largely lost touch with our spiritual heritage. The breakdown in extended family support systems and our general lack of acknowledgement and care of the vulnerable and elderly are also factors.

Humanity's disconnection is also illustrated by our willingness to overlook cruelty to our own species as well as others and the needless destruction of natural resources on our quest for faster, cheaper and unhealthier food options, physical comfort and technological advancement. Our inability to meditate, still our minds and separate from high speed lifestyles that keep us in fight or flight patterns and running on adrenalin and cortisol, our over-exposure to all things traumatic, distressing and violent through our news and all forms of media; all these and more have led us to a culture of insensitivity and unconsciousness.

> *"Quiet minds can't be perplexed or frightened, but go on in fortune or misfortune at their own private pace, like a clock during a thunderstorm"*
>
> Robert Louis Stevenson

Essentially, if you wish to discover the elusive X factor that hides within, you need to place greater importance on the value and sanctity of your inner space. It is nigh on impossible to discover a powerful, grounded and stable sense of self if you are constantly and unconsciously numbing and distracting yourself with self-destructive behaviours in order to make the world you live in bearable.

If you look closely at someone who exudes the X factor, who is charismatic to the point of magnetism, you will notice that they have attached themselves not to objects, people or things but to an idea, a philosophy or a dream. They are not running away from reality, they are creating a new version. People who possess the X factor are always moving towards something that is intangible and often difficult to explain. They have identified and connected to their inner or unconscious drive and are living their lives *on purpose.*

If you wish to have a strong sense of self, you need to access your intuition, unplug yourself from the internet and plug yourself into a universal and less tangible database. To fully grasp whether or not you have value in the world, to recognise your untapped ability and to determine your potential are all issues that ultimately are your concern and yours alone. The bad news is, nobody is going to discover or celebrate your potential until you do. The good news is, nobody is going to discover or celebrate your potential until you do.

If you feel you have something to offer the world, you want to be discovered so you may deliver your offering and be acclaimed for sharing your gift. However until you yourself have dug deep and uncovered the diamond in the rough, you will remain unfulfilled and uncertain of your value. You are not going to discover your value or your worth by purely watching television or staring at a screen, nor are you going to discover it through any purchase, relationship or material gain.

The discovery of your path, your potential and your worth is entirely up to you and depends on your *daily* choices and actions. If you feel undervalued, misunderstood, mistreated or misjudged then you have not yet discovered your own value nor realised your own potential. How can you feel mistreated or low in self-worth if you have connected to your essence and formed a loving and close working relationship with yourself? The only way you can feel rejected and unimportant is if you have created a sense of rejection and lack deep in your core and reinforced it through your thoughts, words and actions.

Does this mean that people who have discovered their *way* or their value in the world are immune to being misjudged, mistreated or misunderstood? No, absolutely not. In fact people who have found their way are often the target of all sorts of attacks, slights of character, innuendos and attempts to bully and demean. Michael Schwandt's story is a clear demonstration of this. The difference is they don't notice, or pay little attention, because they

> *"If you wish to find, you must search. Rarely does a good idea interrupt you"*
>
> Jim Rohn

are too busy following their own path. Their focus is on their dreams, their goals and the opportunities that the future holds. They have accessed their X factor.

So how do we reconnect with our sense of self and understanding your purpose? The first method is to meditate and/or pray regularly. Whether you are spiritually inclined or not, there is no question that meditation and the ability to control and still the mind has enormous emotional, physiological and psychological benefits. If you choose to pray instead of meditate, make sure that you leave a space within your prayer routine for listening as well as actively praying.

You don't have to meditate for hours or go into a deep Zen-like state. Start with five minutes morning and night and develop from there as you begin to experience the benefits. Be sure to keep a pad and pen handy to write down any inspiration or guidance. Undoubtedly you will begin to see, hear and feel differently once you have begun a regular meditation or prayer practice.

Secondly, exercise in a way that works for you, stretch, eat fresh and nourishing foods and drink plenty of fresh chemical-free water. If you wish to feel confident and full of self-esteem, you need to demonstrate to yourself that you are worth it. You will also feel happier and better able to cope with the challenges life throws at you if you have placed your well-being as a high priority.

"If every eight-year-old in the world were taught meditation, we would eliminate violence from the world within one generation"

Dalai Lama

"When you master yourself, you master the world"

The Biggest Bully

*"Tell the person who bullies you "It's over",
and walk away from the mirror"*

Paula Pell

The irony of the bullying cycle is that your greatest adversary and the most significant and hurtful bully you will ever meet, is *YOU*. No one can *force* you to feel anything. People can physically dominate you but not one single person on this planet can force you to feel sad, angry, hurt, disappointed, unworthy, lacking or unimportant. All those feelings are yours and yours alone.

If you are being bullied psychologically or emotionally you have choices, freedom and power. You may choose to access support networks and organisations including friends, family and mentors; however the control of your feelings and thoughts about this situation lies entirely with you.

You can, if you so wish, lay your painful story to rest in this moment. If you *choose* to reach deep inside yourself and decide to see yourself as important, special, worthy and loved, then so be it. Change happens in an instant. Just as trauma can change lives in an instant, overcoming a traumatic situation can change your life for the better just as fast. Light-bulb moments are so called because of the speed with which the change occurs. We all have the possibility to experience our own light-bulb moments throughout life. No one can 'give' you feelings and no one can 'take' them away. The choice is always yours.

Regardless of the intensity or ugliness of the situation you are facing, you can choose to see it as a logical process, a problem to be solved, a riddle to be unravelled or a challenge to be overcome. If you choose *NOT* to believe that you are a victim and so don't need to mould yourself to please another, you can focus your attention on the important matter of extricating yourself from your uncomfortable circumstances. You move from victim to problem solver

"You can chain me, you can torture me, you can even destroy this body, but you will never imprison my mind"

Mahatma Gandhi

in an instant. Instead of focusing on the problem, you can choose to focus on the possible solutions and get moving.

If you choose in this moment to forgive yourself, your frailties, mistakes and failures, forgive others their frailties, mistakes and failures, and see the true beauty of you that lives in your heart of hearts, you will then be able to see the value and potential you bring to this world. All external adversaries will pale in comparison when you recognise that the biggest bully you ever had was hidden in your thinking. It is indeed as simple as that.

> "Bullies are victims who are lashing out.
> Victims are bullies who bully themselves"

Twists and Turns - *Matthew's Story*

"It is better to travel well than to arrive"

Buddha

An Olympic gold-medal-winning diver, Matthew Mitcham, produced the highest scoring dive in Olympic history to win the 10-metre platform event at the 2008 Beijing Olympic Games. In doing so he became Australia's first male diving gold-medallist since Dick Eve in 1924. Despite this stellar achievement Matthew left the sport struggling with addiction to methamphetamine and depression.

His autobiography *Twists and Turns* depicts his journey into and out of depression. Matthew also performs in a musical comedy cabaret show based on his life story. Matthew has bounced back from his bouts of depression, is drug-free and has re-energised his successful diving career. Along with his Olympic gold, he now holds six Commonwealth Games silver medals and a Commonwealth Games gold for the 10-metre synchronised diving in Glasgow in 2014.

Matthew shares his story of triumph over trauma and depicts powerfully the struggle that occurs for people who are battling low confidence and self-esteem. His story demonstrates how no amount of external validation or success can overcome the inner dialogue we tell ourselves and how focusing purely on external validation fails to deliver comfort or satisfaction.

I trudged through half of my teenage years with depression, not doing anything or telling anyone about it because I saw it as a weakness and so was deeply, deeply ashamed. Instead, I resorted to self-harm in a bid to manage my feelings. I thought it worked, too. In my mind, the issue was dealt with and I could move on. I didn't realise I was just postponing the problem.

Diving had a large part to play in my depression. I saw diving as my only opportunity to be the best in the world at something, the panacea for all my problems, the antidote for my low self-esteem, the way to get people to like me. I put all my eggs in one basket with diving, yet I despised sacrificing so much for it and forcing myself to do something I hated, five hours a day, six days a week. I felt like I had no other option because I hadn't acquired any other skills.

Unfortunately it wasn't until I was too miserable to bear it any longer that I did anything about it, which is often the way, isn't it? I retired from diving at the ripe old age of 18 with absolutely no intention of ever returning to the sport. I didn't face my problems, I ran away from them, spending too much time in seedy nightclubs and taking too many party drugs. It took me six months to stop hating the sport, and another three months to start missing it.

That's when my current coach, a Mexican man named Chava Sobrino, sent me an SMS saying, "If you ever want to start diving again, I'll always have a place in my squad in Sydney for you". It was the way it was worded... "If you ever"... nurturing, not pushy, not what I was used to. I knew this was the man who would look after me, who cared for my welfare as a human being more than as an athlete.

One of the other reasons I was not as happy diving in Brisbane was because I didn't feel entirely comfortable in my own skin within my training squad. I had started diving at such a young age, much too young to have established my sexuality, never felt comfortable enough to come out because I felt that would be admitting I had been somehow lying to everybody for the preceding five years. I believe holding this aspect of my identity back caused more problems than it solved, because the other athletes in my squad knew I wasn't being forthright with them and there were consequently trust issues.

When I moved to Sydney I made the conscious decision that I was going to, for the first time, be absolutely 100% open and honest with everyone I met. This was the perfect opportunity for a fresh start. While at times I may have been perhaps a little **too** upfront for some people, I found that on the whole, people interacted with me in a much more open way. Training partners, coaches, work colleagues, divers from other countries, strangers... everyone. Since making that decision I have not had one single homophobic experience. In fact, I've had quite the opposite reaction.

I believe that's because when someone hides aspects of themselves, people sense it and they don't know where the boundaries are because they don't know what the obstacle is. When they know the terrain, they know how to navigate it, making for better interaction. Since becoming open and comfortable about my sexuality, I have never had more straight mates. At competitions the boys make me laugh when they get all possessive over me amongst each other... apparently it has become cool to have a platonic gay friend in some circles.

Being able to be true to myself and being accepted for it had a profound effect on my self-esteem. When I moved to Sydney, there was only 15 months to go until the Beijing Olympic Games. Not ideal timing after having had almost a year off. My goal was just to make the team for Beijing and then make my big gold-medal-winning performance in London. I trained with so much passion and intensity. For the first time in a long while I was diving because I wanted to, not because I felt I had to. I was really happy. In Beijing I became the Gold Medal Olympic champion in the 10 metre platform, and received the highest single-dive score in Olympic history.

Perhaps naively, I thought I was fixed. I was happy, successful and popular. But it wasn't enough for me. My self-esteem needed more bolstering. When I looked on the International Diving website at the world rankings, I saw that I was number two in the world, as earlier in the year the Chinese diver had won more events than I had. All I could think about was seeing myself splashed across the face of every newspaper: 'Australian diver, one-hit wonder', and 'Matthew Mitcham, splash in the pan'.

The motivation to keep training after Beijing was actually quite negative. My self-esteem was so fragile that I had become completely dependent on positive feedback from external sources, like the fans on my social networking pages and my coach during training sessions. My perception of my worth was measured in numbers: how many Facebook and Twitter followers I had, how many tens I got from the judges, how much money I had in the bank; none of which was ever enough when I compared myself to other people. Even when I was ranked number one in the world in 2010, it wasn't enough. I was still empty.

After that, I struggled with injuries for the next year-and-a-half. I couldn't train, I couldn't compete. I lost all sources of that external positive feedback that I had become so reliant upon, and it was no surprise that I went straight back to the last coping mechanisms I had as a teenager: drugs and alcohol. I felt down, and reached for something to make myself feel better. Then I felt worse. So I did the same thing again and again, perpetuating and reinforcing the cycle each time. I knew these short-term solutions were exacerbating my blues, but they were the most effective tool I had for changing my feelings at the time, because I had never addressed any of the problems I had as a teen, preferring to numb myself instead.

Asking anyone for help was the very last resort. I felt more ashamed than ever that I had let myself get to this point, and felt my problems were unjustified. It wasn't until it got bad enough that I decided I couldn't fix this one by myself, that I reached out for help. That was when I realised I had been suffering unnecessarily for years. I was 22 before I discovered I didn't have all the answers. There were people who knew better than me. These were the people I reached out to.

I started seeing a psychologist twice a week to help me make head and tail of what was going on. That's when I learnt that drinking and drugging were a symptom rather than a cause of my depression; when I learnt I had such poor self-esteem; when I learnt how dependent I had become on all these external things to make myself feel better. I learnt that self-esteem should come from within and external positive reinforcement should just be a bonus. I learnt that my mental health was my own responsibility, and that being proactive about improving my mental health was also a way to improve my self-esteem.

All this stuff didn't come straight away. I continued seeing the psychologist twice a week for the entire year in the lead-up to the London Games, to help deal with the other pressures that were affecting me. The main one was the expectation to defend my Olympic title, which I was finding was becoming increasingly counter-productive to my preparation. 'Don't worry about it' and 'who cares' would have been as effective as telling someone who's having a panic attack to 'just calm down'. So I followed through the worst case scenario over and over again with the psychologist, exploring what it would mean if I didn't defend my title, what the worst that could happen would be. I eventually realised that I would still have the things that were most important to me, and I would be okay even if that scenario were to play out.

That's not to say I had any less anxiety about that worst case scenario playing out, leading all the way up to the Olympic Games in London. In fact, even after I messed up my last dive in London, making me miss out on the finals altogether, all of that 'stinking thinking' hit me like a ton of bricks. I started bawling my eyes out right there on the pool deck, with all the cameras right up in my face streaming my tears and snot to television screens all over the world. I hadn't done it; I had sabotaged myself with all my self-destructive behaviours; my family had spent so much money to come here to watch me. These were just a few of the things that were ruminating around my head and making me sadder and sadder. But within just five minutes, I consciously stopped the counter-productive thinking and pulled myself together, since I had to do the walk of shame through the media zone. No, I didn't **do** my best, but I **tried** my best. I could not have done more in the lead-up to the Games because of my injuries; in fact, I should have done less to prevent all those re-injuries. Yes, my family spent a lot of money, but they wanted to. And I hadn't defended my title, but I was okay.

It only took me about six hours to actually believe the stuff I was saying to the media. This was the point where I realised that all the work I did on my mental health in the lead-up to the London Games had actually paid off. I didn't have a great big medal hanging around my neck, but I felt like a much happier, healthier, more wholesome person, which actually meant more to me. I haven't stopped seeing the psychologist since London 2012, because I think the investment in my mental health has definitely been worth it. The skills I'm developing to help me become a happier person are invaluable. I can't stress enough the importance of reaching out as a first resort, not a last one.

Matthew Mitcham
Olympian
www.twistsandturns.com.au

The Means To Attain A Happy Life

Martial, the things that do attain
The happy life, be these, I find:
The riches left, not got with pain;
The fruitful ground, the quiet mind;

The equal friend, no grudge, no strife;
No charge of rule, nor governance;
Without disease, the healthful life;
The household of continuance;

The mean diet, no delicate fare;
True wisdom join'd with simpleness;
The night discharged of all care,
Where wine the wit may not oppress;

The faithful wife, without debate;
Such sleeps as may beguile the night.
Contented with thine own estate;
Ne wish for Death, ne fear his might.

Henry Howard,
Earl of Surrey 1517-1547

All by Myself

"To those who doubted, thank you.
You have made me strong"

Connection is a basic human need which causes emotional distress or disturbance when unfulfilled. This need for connection can override common sense when it comes to relationships and we at times blindly seek to connect with people who have little or nothing in common with us. This is particularly prevalent in schools where we can find ourselves surrounded by people with whom we do not feel aligned.

At one time or another in your lifetime you will probably find yourself alone and for some this can be challenging to the extreme. There is enormous value in learning techniques and strategies which enable you to feel a sense of connection regardless of your external experience.

It is precisely within this space of aloneness that your creativity and inspiration lives. It is necessary for you to disconnect from the drama that surrounds you in order to reconnect with your inner world and discover what it is you are here for. Aloneness is important, valuable and healing. If you are feeling left out or rejected, take it as an opportunity to find out more about yourself and figure out what it is you would really like to be doing with your life.

The irony of aloneness is that once you have found a way of making peace with being alone and found your happy, creative, connected place, it becomes increasingly difficult to find space to *actually* be alone. People who have learned to connect to themselves at a deep level automatically become magnetic to others.

> *"I live in that solitude which is painful in youth, but delicious in the years of maturity"*
>
> Albert Einstein

Albert Einstein understood that people who are different in some way often feel isolated regardless of their environment, *especially* when they are young. His life is a demonstration of the power that can be drawn from solitude, sometimes interpreted as rejection, and the creative value it can ultimately bring. Celebrate your uniqueness and the differences you see in others; they are humanity's greatest gift and hide seeds of greatness.

> *"The art of being happy lies in the power of extracting happiness from common things"*
>
> Henry Ward Beecher

Be Present

*"Realise deeply that the present moment is all you have. Make the
NOW the primary focus of your life"*

Eckhart Tolle

A man sat at a metro station in Washington DC and started to play the violin. He beautifully executed six Bach pieces over about 45 minutes. During that time, since it was rush hour, several thousand people went through the station, most of them on their way to work.

After a few minutes a middle-aged man noticed the musician. He slowed his pace, stopped for a few seconds and then hurried on. A moment later, the violinist received his first tip: a woman threw a dollar into his open violin case and continued to walk. A few moments later, a man stopped and leaned against a wall to listen but soon looked at his watch and moved on.

The one who paid the most attention was a young boy. His mother hurried him along but he stopped to look at the violinist. Eventually the mother became more insistent and the child walked on, turning his head all the time. This was repeated by several other children. All the parents, without exception, forced them to move on.

In the 45 minutes the musician played, only six commuters stopped. About 20 gave him money but continued walking. He collected $32. When he finished playing and silence took over, no one noticed it. No one applauded, nor was there any recognition.

The violinist was Joshua Bell, one of the finest classical musicians in the world, playing some of the most elegant music ever written on one of the most valuable violins ever made. Two days before his playing in the subway, Joshua Bell sold out at a theatre in Boston where the seats averaged $100 each.

This was organised by the Washington Post in April 2007 as part of a social experiment into people's perception, taste and priorities. It highlights the plight we now face. We have literally become a human 'race', failing to stop, failing to absorb, failing to experience and failing to notice. We are largely disconnected from our surroundings, from beauty and each other. Our technology, our drive and our life choices have placed us in the unenviable position of being unable to live in harmony with our surroundings, unable to connect to our environment and perhaps, unable to experience the joys of life. We are lost in the story of us, in the hustle and bustle of life, in the never-ending bombardment and overstimulation of our senses, and the consequences are disturbing.

Eckhart Tolle in his book *The Power of Now* illustrates beautifully the intrinsic value that can be found in letting go of the past, no longer projecting into the future and embracing the present moment. This simple practice alone is enough to liberate you from painful patterns if you are in the habit of dwelling on the past and feeling anxious or worried about the future.

Dwelling on the past and projecting into the future is our greatest source of discontent and pain. Pay attention to this moment, for indeed it is all you ever have. At any given moment in time we are able to find something joyful to focus on and something painful to relive or imagine. The willingness to focus on fearful, sad or anxious thoughts is a habit many of us fall into. We are largely unconscious of our ability to govern thoughts and can consequently live tortured lives. You are not *receiving* thoughts randomly selected and thrown your way. You are *creating* thoughts and as such are the controller. You may say, 'This thought just keeps coming into my head and I can't get rid of it'. Well actually you can, and it is a very easy process.

> "*The great arises out of small things that are honoured and cared for. Everybody's life really consists of small things. Greatness is a mental abstraction and a favourite fantasy of the ego. The paradox is that the foundation for greatness is the honouring of the small things of the present moment instead of pursuing the idea of greatness*"
>
> Eckhart Tolle

Eckhart Tolle teaches us that the easiest way to get rid of an unpleasant or unwanted thought is to repeat to yourself 'I am thinking' which puts you in the position of observer of the thought and immediately breaks the flow. This can also be used to clear your mind when meditating. An equally helpful alternative is to repeat out loud or in your head, 'Delete, delete, delete, cancel, cancel, cancel' which is a highly effective way to instruct or programme your unconscious mind to choose an alternate thought. With children, encourage them to focus on something pleasant, something uplifting or fun as a replacement for the negative thought.

Your unconscious mind listens to you as would an eight-year-old child. It takes instruction and believes everything you tell it. Importantly your unconscious mind does not differentiate between you and another and as such will interpret EVERYTHING you say as personal to you. Remember this the next time you decide to criticise or belittle another. A little tip would be to be very conscious and careful about the thoughts and words you use from now on; your unconscious mind is listening intently and with great interest.

"Life is what happens to you while you're busy making other plans"

John Lennon

Waiting for Salvation

It rained for days and days and there was a terrific flood. The water rose so high that a man was forced to climb on top of his roof and sit in the rain. As the waters rose, a man in a rowboat came up to the house and told him to get in. "No thank you, God will save me," he said, and the man in the rowboat rowed away.

The waters rose to the edge of the roof and still the man sat there until another rowboat came by and another man told him to get in. "No thank you, God will save me," he said again, and the man rowed away.

The waters covered the house and the man was forced to sit on his chimney as the rain poured down. A helicopter came by and another man urged him to get in or he would drown. "No thank you," the man said again, "God will save me!"

After much begging and pleading the man in the helicopter gave up and flew away. The waters rose above the chimney and the man drowned and went to heaven, where he met God.

"Lord, I don't understand," the man said to Him, frustrated. "The waters rose higher and higher and I waited hours for You to save me but You didn't! Why?"

The Lord just shook his head and said, "What are you talking about? I sent two boats and a helicopter!"

Origin Unknown

Although as a race we have a consummate ability to complain and lament our situation, we are also particularly skilled at remaining stuck in problems for the longest of times. For some, sadly, remaining stuck can last a lifetime. There is a lamentable lack of personal responsibility in changing one's own circumstances. This includes the thinking that the responsibility lies with God or some other spiritual being. This kind of thinking does not produce creative and empowered life experience.

Waiting for God to show up and take care of things, make your body fit and healthy, give you instant access to knowledge that will lead to a great career, or to generously bestow a million dollars on you is not a productive way to live. Ask yourself the question, what am I doing with my energy, my opportunities and my gifts? What exactly am I waiting for?

In the book *The Essence of Happiness* the Dalai Lama explains:

> "Although one's experiences are a consequence of one's past deeds, that does not mean that the individual has no choice or that there is no room for initiative to change… One should not become passive and try to excuse oneself from having to take personal initiative on the grounds that everything is a result of Karma, because if one understands the concept of Karma properly, one will understand that Karma means 'action'… So what type of future will come about, to a large extent, lies within our own hands in the present. It will be determined by the kind of initiatives that we take now."

There is more to life than simply living at the mercy of external, random, unseen and uncontrollable powers at play. To be able to achieve your goals in dreams you will need to be in an empowered and resourceful state and be conscious of your ability to manage and master your destiny.

Everything that has happened in your life has been as a result of choices, some of them conscious, some of them unconscious. You are not at the capricious mercy of some random cosmic practical joke and can begin the journey into self-mastery and open yourself to the knowledge that you are indeed creative and unlimited. Apart from being on a path to independence and personal power, it is far more fun than sitting on the couch, eating junk food, buying lottery tickets and complaining how hard life is.

"There is a family of us who have this yearning for a kind of excellence that we can manifest every day of our lives, a family who wants to believe we're not pawns, we're not victims on this planet, that knows we have the power within us here and now to change the world we see around us!"

Richard Bach

In order to find solutions, focus on the solving and not on the problem. Again, the question is not 'why are these things happening?', the question is 'what can I now change?' We spend a great deal of time focusing on and energising problems. Our obsessive desire to focus on problems and disasters locks us in a never-ending cycle of shifting from one dilemma to the next. Is it any wonder that so many people are struggling with anxiety and depression with the deluge of images of death, violence, desolation or famous falls from grace, throughout the media? We need to be reporting solutions and focusing ourselves in that direction if we are to make the necessary social shift in consciousness that will precipitate change.

"Odie, let's talk effort versus return here. You know, you can still lead a pointless life without all that running around"

Garfield (Jim Davis)

Build Your Inner Muscle – *Tracey Carmichael*

"Pleasure is always derived from something outside you, whereas joy arises from within"

Eckhart Tolle

Tracey Carmichael is one of our official *From Bullied to Brilliant* coaches, is trained in NLP and is adept in the transformative use of language. Tracey is the author of *Happy Mind Formula* and is also a wellness and mind-set coach, NLP and Timeline Therapy® practitioner, strategic intervention coach and yoga instructor. She brings to these roles 15 years' experience in the wellness industry as a natural therapist. Here Tracey shares with us her deep understanding of the connection between mental, physical and emotional health and well-being.

In tough times; when life challenges us both mentally and physically, it is important to find inner strength; to build our inner muscle to cope with anything life throws at us.

A person who has inner strength has great capability for facing challenges. Being strong means having the resources, mental skills and physical capabilities to confront difficulties of all kinds. When you are strong you have the energy and inner strength to take action in your own life.

When our inner strength is low or non-existent it is easy to feel victimised in our own lives. We feel powerless against the actions of others; we feel alienated and alone.

When we are unhappy with life or feel victimised, it is easy to blame others for our circumstances and make excuses for our loss of personal power. We want to believe that someone else is responsible for the situation we are in. We blame our partners, work colleagues, children, parents, friends or even the place we live for a life we are not happy with.

It is this action of blame that strips us of our personal power to take action and move forward. We make ourselves redundant in our own lives.

For years I have pondered the question 'Why do some people cope and some don't?'

I see people who have endured huge challenges and great loss in their lives who are happy and I see people who have had it relatively easy, seem to have everything and are unhappy.

In a nutshell, happy and strong people have daily rituals that serve them.

Daily rituals are good habits such as a healthy diet, daily exercise, self-care, self-love, purpose and feeding the mind positive information. It is these daily rituals that directly affect our physiology and determine whether we are healthy or unhealthy, both mentally and physically.

Physiology refers to the mechanical, physical, bioelectrical, and biochemical functions of the organs and the cells of which we are composed. And our physiology directly affects our state, which refers to how we feel emotionally each day; happy, sad, angry, depressed, or anxious to name a few.

It is our state that then directly affects our behaviour, which is how we cope, operate and communicate in the world. Our behaviour determines our relationships, who and what we attract into our lives and how successful we are.

You invariably attract people into your life who are in harmony with your thoughts and emotions. When you are demonstrating negative behaviours and thoughts you attract people who are also like that. When you make new choices and include more positive activities into your lifestyle, you will also attract positive like-minded people and a whole new cycle begins. Like attracts like and you will find yourself in a continuous loop of positivity. You will have broken the cycle and given yourself the opportunity to experience a great life.

Happy, positive and successful people weren't born that way; they work on themselves daily to achieve this result and it all starts with daily rituals.

There are many daily rituals we can incorporate into our lives; however, I feel that there are four main ones. If we want to be in driver's seat of our own lives then it is important to commit to a healthy diet, daily exercise, meditation and personal development.

Diet

When we feel disempowered we often reach for highly processed comfort foods. While these foods may give us instant gratification, it is their long-term effect that requires mentioning. Foods high in simple carbohydrates such as wheat, gluten and sugar have a direct effect on mood and coping mechanisms. These foods combined make up simple carbohydrates and cause a dramatic spike in blood sugar levels and serotonin.

Serotonin is considered a 'happy' hormone. It greatly influences an overall sense of well-being as it helps regulate moods, temper anxiety, and relieve depression.

The rise in serotonin is the reason we feel instantly better when we eat these foods. The downside though is that because these foods enter the bloodstream very quickly they also leave it very quickly, causing the blood sugar levels to fall dramatically, along with serotonin levels. This cycle of high and low blood-sugar levels causes a roller coaster of high and lows in mood and of course affects our coping mechanisms.

This cycle can easily be broken by eliminating highly processed foods from our diet and replacing them with lean protein, fresh fruit and vegetables and nuts and seeds. Making this simple change to our diet will help us to lose weight, strengthen our bodies, stabilise moods and improve coping mechanisms.

Exercise

Exercise is an amazing way to build internal and external muscle. The idea that regular exercise can improve our coping mechanisms is not new. Hippocrates was the first Western physician to prescribe this treatment 2,500 years ago and doctors have been recommending it ever since. When the body is fit and strong, so is the mind.

Often when people are not coping they are prescribed anti-depressants to help them through difficult times. Research from Duke University in North Carolina shows that exercising three times per week can be just as effective as medication in helping people cope. In some studies people were no longer considered clinically depressed after incorporating regular exercise into their lives.

Studies show that both aerobic exercise and resistance training

"The human body is the best picture of the human soul"

Ludwig Wittgenstein

help to increase and maintain serotonin levels in the body. Exercise also provides a distraction from the negative thought and behavioural patterns. It keeps the focus on the positive and helps us to connect with positive like-minded people, which in turn boosts confidence and self-esteem.

Meditation

Our thoughts directly affect our behaviour and coping mechanisms and therefore need to be addressed daily. When we are not coping with life, our thoughts are often negative and self-destructive. The way we perceive ourselves and the world we live in can be very dark.

Fortunately this process can be easily turned around through meditation. Meditation is a universal practice which is becoming increasingly popular in the West to quieten the mind, reduce stress and heal the body, mind and spirit. It is a system anyone can master, where thought, contemplation and reflection are used to improve physical and emotional well-being. 15 to 20 minutes per day in meditation or quiet contemplation can greatly improve our coping mechanisms and help to build inner muscle.

Personal Development

The brain is just like any other muscle or organ in the body; it needs to be nourished and exercised in order to function optimally. It becomes stronger through use and weaker through disuse. A healthy mind is one that is constantly exposed to new challenges and adventures. When your mind is healthy you think faster, understand concepts more easily, prevent brain disease and most importantly, feel good about your life and who you are.

Personal development in the form of reading, workshops or therapy allows you to explore who you are, where you are in life, where you want to go and how to get there. It allows you to stand apart from yourself and explore your thoughts, motives, actions and behaviours.

Through personal development you learn to implement change by tapping into your intuition and inner wisdom. You also learn to communicate more effectively and develop a set of tools to use in any negative or complex situations in life.

When you have an awareness of the cause and effect of where you are at in your life and realise that no one is coming to rescue you, you can propel yourself into taking action. Action means *doing; it means making an effort and making changes. Action means work, discipline and commitment and this all starts with implementing your daily rituals to build your inner muscle.*

Tracey Carmichael
Happy Mind Coach and Yoga Instructor
www.happymindstudio.com

The Two Wolves

One evening an old Cherokee told his grandson about a battle that goes on inside people.

He said, "My son, the battle is between two wolves inside us all."

"One is Evil – It is anger, envy, jealousy, sorrow, regret, greed, arrogance, self-pity, guilt, resentment, inferiority, lies, false pride, superiority, and ego."

"The other is Good – It is joy, peace, love, hope, serenity, humility, kindness, benevolence, empathy, generosity, truth, compassion and faith."

The grandson thought about it for a minute and then asked his grandfather: "Which wolf wins?"

The old Cherokee simply replied, "The one you feed."

Cherokee Legend

SECTION 4

RAISING EMPOWERED CHILDREN

The Butterfly and the Cocoon

A man found a cocoon of a butterfly. One day a small opening appeared. He sat and watched the butterfly for several hours as it struggled to squeeze its body through the tiny hole. Then it stopped, as if it couldn't go further.

So the man decided to help the butterfly. He took a pair of scissors and snipped off the remaining bits of cocoon. The butterfly emerged easily but it had a swollen body and shrivelled wings.

The man continued to watch it, expecting that any minute the wings would enlarge and expand enough to support the body. Neither happened! In fact the butterfly spent the rest of its life crawling around. It was never able to fly.

What the man in his kindness and haste did not understand was that the restricting cocoon and the struggle required by the butterfly to get through the opening was a way of forcing the fluid from the body into the wings so that it would be ready for flight once that was achieved.

Sometimes struggles are exactly what we need in our lives. Going through life with no obstacles would cripple us. We will not be as strong as we could have been and we would never fly.

Author Unknown

There was a young man who sought help from a counsellor. He felt he needed to resolve the resentment he felt towards his controlling mother as he had never felt loved. When asked what exactly his mother did that indicated her lack of love for him, he said that as a boy every day she picked out his clothes and laid them on his bed. He had no choice what he wore and he had always resented this. He felt this was a clear sign that she didn't love him or respect him as an individual. The counsellor thought long and hard and then said to the young man, "It's funny, I thought my mother didn't love me because she never picked out my clothes and laid them on my bed."

"Those who are free of resentful thoughts surely find peace"

Buddha

When interpreting events and circumstances around you, be mindful of the need to expand your thinking beyond the most obvious choices. Parents and spouses show their love in a variety of ways and all are open to interpretation. Seeming disinterest can be an inability to express emotion, anger can stem from fearful protective thoughts, controlling behaviours can be a desire to feel needed and relevant and bullying can be a cry for help.

If in fact we are all making everything up in our heads, doesn't it make sense to make up the best possible story?

"Love is working for the development of the potential of being"

Eugene Halliday

Unravelling the Knots

"It's not that I'm so smart, it's just that I stay with problems longer"

Albert Einstein

Parenting as a rule is complex, fraught with communication breakdowns and difficult to navigate. For most if not all parents, given we are so gloriously imperfect, the chances of making mistakes and experiencing storms as we sail the HMAS Madhouse through uncharted waters, ranks incredibly high.

In today's world the job of parenting now comes with the added bonus of information, technology and activity overload. Many families are headed by full-time working parents so it is no wonder that the word *overwhelm* flows so easily in conversation. Schools appear to be blithely unaware of this predicament, sending a barrage of paperwork and requests for community support to an already overstretched and fraught working parent.

After-school activities are a stretch. Families with more children than parents are faced with a sometimes impossible task of chaperoning their prodigy to differing and multiple events, not to mention paying for them. I once had an in-depth chat with the registrar at soccer sign up. She explained to me very calmly and politely how much the club depended on volunteers and how little the joining fee actually covered. They kindly allowed us to use their balls and their pitch but the rest appeared to be more or less up to us. I almost ran screaming from the room, but of course I didn't. My son had only one shot at being six and I certainly didn't want to be the reason his international soccer career never saw the light of day.

"Life's not about waiting for the storm to pass. It's about learning to dance in the rain"

Vivian Greene

If evenings aren't full enough of the regular stuff of home life: homework, reading folders, sight words, maths and word games; in the midst of the chaos come the school assignments. I don't know about you, but my parents *NEVER* helped me with an assignment. *Never, ever!* I feel like I'm the one getting the homework these days. Flashback to being punished for staring out of the window…How I long for school holidays…

There are emotional pressures, financial pressures, relationship pressures, the pressure of running a (relatively) functioning home, whilst dodging a never ending technological 'look at me' barrage from social media, emails, SMS, and phone. There are pets to care for, cars to maintain and a garden which grows like an invasion of the Triffids. Friends in need, friends whose names you can barely remember, mail, bills, notices, renewals, tax, it never stops.

When, and more importantly *if* you finally flop down on the couch in a gibbering incoherent heap, there is the world's greatest indoctrinator and hypnotist, the television, bombarding our senses with stressful and dramatic images, selling products we don't want or need and lulling us into an imaginary world, skilfully created by media management and advertisers banking on the fact that we are too tired to think for ourselves or do anything productive to help us step off the merry-go-round of modern day life. Is it any wonder that many parents are struggling to maintain their sanity?

"He hoped and prayed that there wasn't an afterlife. Then he realised there was a contradiction involved here and merely hoped that there wasn't an afterlife"

Douglas Adams

"Only two things are infinite, the universe and human stupidity, and I'm not sure about the former"

Albert Einstein

Needless to say, despite the pressures and perceived sense of inadequacy, as a parent or carer you still have the unique and powerful ability to instil in your children unconscious patterns that they may choose to operate from for the rest of their lives. Being a 'good enough' parent is a subjective and illusive ideal that generally escapes most mortals. A rule of thumb could be that successful parenting depends less on your ability to deliver the latest and greatest, and far more on the importance and significance you place on mental and emotional well-being, including your own.

In the quest to become a super-parent you may find yourself faced at times with ungrateful and thoughtless progeny. Children are not renowned for their ability to empathise with the plight of a frazzled and frustrated parent. Ironically, it can be when you are at your most vulnerable that some children, finding themselves no longer the centre of attention, seek to provoke using negative behaviours. Children can have a keen sense of weakness and are ready to jump on you if you waver. If you need some time to regroup, don't be hard on yourself. Being a parent is not easy and you can rest assured that your children will be able to find fault with your system regardless.

"He was a dreamer, a thinker, a speculative philosopher...
or, as his wife would have it, an idiot"

Douglas Adams

Why Yelling Doesn't Work

"I suppose leadership at one time meant muscles;
but today it means getting along with people"

Mahatma Gandhi

Father: *"My children will not suffer fools gladly. I am raising strong children who know the difference between right and wrong, who know how to stand up for themselves and will never be pushed around."*

Questioner: *"How are you doing that?"*

Father: *"I am going to make sure they never put a foot wrong while they live under my roof. I rule with an iron fist and an iron will. Nobody gets the better of me and my children will learn the same way I did. The hard way."*

Questioner: *"So you are going to push them around and force your version of right and wrong on them and they had better submit or else…?"*

Father: *"Yes."*

Questioner: *"But I thought you said your children don't suffer fools…?"*

As we progress in our understanding of the dominance/submissive pattern that exists in many human interactions, we need to look closely at how we programme our children from an early age. We live in a society which suggests that bullying in the school and workplace is unacceptable yet defends the right to use abuse and corporal punishment in the home. Diminishing or subjugating another is a violation of human rights and corporal punishment of children is considered a crime in around 37 countries around the world.

Source: www.endcorporalpunishment.org/pages/research/prohibited.html

"Anger and intolerance are the enemies of correct understanding"

Mahatma Gandhi

My father's generation were not so au fait with parenting with confidence and self-esteem in mind, and even if they were, would have almost certainly dismissed it out of hand. Many men of his era were still struggling with the concept of Women's Lib and did not consider raising children as something that required great thought. Some were under the impression that boys needed toughening up through force and harshness for them to become *real* men. For many children, including my father, this had unwelcome, painful and sometimes damaging results.

If you prefer the more controlled approach and raise your children to be obedient, submissive and to accept your authority in all things, then be aware that a power for dominion approach programmes children to accept the authority of, and obedience and submission to, another person. This may work well for parents in the early years but consider the repercussions once the child begins to step away from the parental umbrella with a strong unconscious pattern/need to find someone of authority to tell them what to do. That person may well be a school bully, a dominant or aggressive teacher or mentor, or even an abusive future spouse.

This can be especially problematic if the person that they have formed an allegiance to does not actually value or love your child. To raise independent and free-willed children, consider focusing on their innate knowledge and insight and encourage them to value,

"Whatever is begun in anger ends in shame"

Benjamin Franklin

believe in and honour themselves. A strong sense of self-belief, trust in their own inherent intuition and the ability to make good choices are attributes that need to be developed in childhood. You don't beat confidence, self-esteem and personal power into children, you beat it out of them.

The rather glaring flaw in the power for dominion approach is that if you are raising sons with the intention to physically dominate and intimidate them into submission, there is in all likelihood a moment when they will become bigger, stronger and potentially taller than you are. If you are relying on physical presence and strength to get your own way, you may well find yourself backed into a corner, both metaphorically and physically speaking.

This lesson was learned the hard way by a friend of ours with twin sons who at a certain point in time, (probably around the time they grew to over two metres tall) decided that Dad no longer had the physical advantage and promptly picked him up, turned him upside down and told him enough was enough. These young men and their father were thankfully loving, kind and in possession of a remarkably good sense of humour. As a consequence their relationship mutated into one based more on mutual respect and less of the turning people upside down. For many, this is not the case.

Dads, take heed. There are other, far more beneficial ways to care for and raise sons. If you wish to keep your feet on the ground and have a healthy and mutually respectful relationship, improve your communication skills.

> *"When You Choose To Be Pleasant And Positive In The Way You Treat Others, You Have Also Chosen, In Most Cases, How You Are Going To Be Treated By Them"*
>
> Zig Ziglar

Intimidation and dominance can be damaging *even if the intention is loving.* Positive outcomes will be difficult to achieve if a child has been intimidated into either submission (repressed negative emotion) or rebelliousness (expressed negative emotion). Intimidation and dominance tend to bring out two major emotions, fear and anger. If felt strongly, fear and anger can both cause a child to develop hidden resentment, submission or inhibition.

Generally, children do not have the life experience, intuition or wisdom to see past their dominant parents' behaviour. They will find it hard to discover a strong sense of self-worth if they are being regularly intimidated and dominated.

Empowerment, optimism, creativity, enthusiasm and self-worth do not grow from underlying anger or fear. They are the result of a strong sense of self-confidence, of feeling valued, valuable and loved regardless of personality, behaviour or capability.

Many parents' and educators' deepest and most heartfelt intention is to raise children who feel empowered, are full of optimism and have an innate ability to deal with life's challenges. They want children to have a strong sense of self-worth and hold firm the belief that they possess all the information they require to lead full and successful lives. They wish to help children be emotionally strong and independent of spirit, able to attract and create great relationships with people who respect and honour their opinion, beliefs and dreams.

No parent is equipped with all the information or knowledge required to raise a happy and integrated adult. Each child is different, as is each adult. Our interpretations, needs and desires are unique and as such there is no one on this planet who is sufficiently equipped

> *"What good is it to live a life that brings pains?"*
>
> Aeschylus

to teach us all we need to know. Parents, you are off the hook. You are free to allow your children to grow into independent individuals. You are not an expert in your child and you do not have to feel entirely responsible for their happiness and well-being. Now breathe a sigh of relief, stop yelling and get on with enjoying your journey through life together.

These action steps will help you on your way:

- Tell your children you love them, daily
- Turn off your technology and be present with your family as often as possible
- Look directly into their eyes when you speak to them
- Tell them they are unique, powerful, different and glorious in their difference
- Encourage them to trust their gut feelings and believe in themselves even in the face of opposition
- Teach them to follow their dreams and their hearts
- Admit to them you do not have all the answers and that you may sometimes be wrong
- Ask for their forgiveness when you make a mistake
- Hug them whenever possible (or as often as they permit)
- Respect their choices even if you don't like them
- Recognise that at some point in time they may well be able to turn you upside down
- Plan accordingly.

The pathways for dominant or submissive behaviours are initially formed in the home. If you wish to raise empowered and happy kids, then empower and encourage them. Ask their opinion, treat them with respect, admiration and love. They won't be children for long.

"The ideals which have lighted my way, and time after time have given me new courage to face life cheerfully, have been kindness, beauty and truth"

Albert Einstein

On Children

Your children are not your children.
They are the sons and daughters of Life's longing for itself.
They come through you but not from you,
And though they are with you yet they belong not to you.

You may give them your love but not your thoughts,
For they have their own thoughts.
You may house their bodies but not their souls,
For their souls dwell in the house of tomorrow,
which you cannot visit, not even in your dreams.
You may strive to be like them,
but seek not to make them like you.
For life goes not backward nor tarries with yesterday.

You are the bows from which your children
as living arrows are sent forth.
The archer sees the mark upon the path of the infinite,
and He bends you with His might
that His arrows may go swift and far.
Let your bending in the archer's hand be for gladness;
For even as He loves the arrow that flies,
so He loves also the bow that is stable.

Kahlil Gibran

Empowered Education

"Educating the mind without educating the heart is no education at all"

Aristotle

The following story was contributed by a primary school principal working in an underprivileged area with many at-risk children. I feel so blessed to be able to include the story and commend this wonderful lady for her skill, insight, strength and gentleness in dealing with a particularly troubled little boy and the problems that surrounded him. It is heartening to know that our education system harbours such people who are willing to guide and care for our children.

It also highlights our inability to effectively seek out the help we need. Even when every effort has been taken to protect the children, it is primarily the unwillingness of the victim to speak up and seek help that allows the problem to persist and grow to unacceptable levels.

Sam's Story

As principal of the school, I had uncovered a bullying problem with one child, but had a strong feeling that this wasn't the only child Sam had bullied. Firstly I prayed for wisdom—something I always did when I knew I could be on dangerous territory. I then decided to do something I'd never done before and tackle the issue with the whole class, not individuals.

I gathered the grade sevens together in a circle and told them we had a problem we needed to talk through and resolve. I started by going round the circle asking a series of questions.

"Has anything happened to you in grade seven that has made you sad?"

Most of the class said, "Yes".

The next question was, "Can you tell me what made you sad?"

To my horror, a large proportion of the children said, "Bullying".

"Can you tell me what happened—without telling me who did it?"

The experiences they shared with me made me feel incredibly sad—being hit every time they went to the toilet, feeling afraid to be in the corridor on their own in case they were bullied etc.

"I want you to be really brave and tell me who did it. I promise you we'll do something about it."

At this point I stole a look across to Sam, sitting with his head down, shoulders dropped. As we went around the circle, each child said, "I can't, Mrs Jones, I'm too scared."

Then—and I will never forget this moment, as long as I live— the smallest boy in the class, Jim, said, "I'll tell you, Mrs Jones, it was Sam."

Others then took courage and gave me the same name. By this point, Sam had tears streaming down his face. I gently asked the class teacher to take him out of the class and have a talk to him. The next moment was when I knew I'd been successful in what I was trying to achieve in this very tough school.

When asked the question, "Right, grade sevens, what are we going to do now?" little Jim said, "Well, Miss, he's only behaving like he is because somebody's hurt him—we just need to love him, don't we?"

I've got a lump in my throat and tears in my eyes as I remember that moment and I assure you, I couldn't hold back the tears on that day! We went on to devise several strategies and then invited Sam back in to tell him what we'd all decided—in particular that we loved him and wanted him to be happy.

Any principal who says they don't have a bullying problem is operating with their head in the sand. I thought I'd got it sorted with cutting edge anti-bullying policies and sensitive staff, but Sam's story was a real wake-up call!

Along with the home environment, one of the fundamental players in the lifelong game of low confidence and self-esteem is the experience at school. The challenge of raising empowered and inspired children is difficult in schools where rules and restrictions inhibit or even prohibit self-expression, self-determination and independent thinking.

"Wisdom, compassion, and courage are the three universally recognised moral qualities of men"

Confucius

These days many schools are struggling with targets, protocols, standardised testing and increasingly high expectations. Many teachers are overwhelmed and often under-resourced, class sizes are large and the instances of children with learning difficulties or emotional and behavioural problems are climbing, along with the practice of medicating and sedating children.

Teaching children how to be empowered, inspired, forward thinking and emotionally equipped just doesn't make it into the syllabus when even maths and English are at times slipping through the cracks. Teachers are not employed for their ability to teach life skills; they are hired and trained to educate.

Our education system was not originally intended as a free thinking or liberal approach to learning and development, and as such was not designed to encourage behaviour or thinking that falls outside of the planned structure. It is an academic model created by academics, for academics. Sir Ken Robinson, Professor of Arts Education and international advisor on education in the arts to government, believes the education system to be modelled on factory-style production that was born in the Industrial Revolution. More often than not this system, in spite of many

"I believe this passionately: that we don't grow into creativity, we grow out of it. Or rather, we get educated out of it"

Ken Robinson

teachers' efforts, does not encourage people who are less academic, more artistic or practical by nature to feel particularly good about themselves.

"Never believe that a few caring people can't change the world. For, indeed, that's all who ever have"

Margaret Mead

Although intellectual and physical growth is well supported in our current education system, this alone does not equip young people with the ability to manage conflict and rejection. To allow for a broader and more rounded experience, creativity, expression, relationships and life skills must be equally valued and nurtured.

Unless you intend to abdicate responsibility and place your child's emotional well-being in a system that has evidently room for improvement, or you are lucky enough to have your child in a school with an inspired and forward-thinking principal, or some particularly determined teachers, you will have to get on with the job of teaching your child resilience and personal power yourself. Confidence comes from self-belief, from the ability to trust your own instincts, intuitions or gut feelings even when faced with opposition, and the courage to step up and do what is necessary. The best way to teach this to your children, is to demonstrate it in yourself.

"To those of you who received honours, awards and distinctions, I say well done. And to the C students, I say you, too, can be president of the United States."

George W. Bush

The Benefits of Bullying

"You can't climb a mountain if it is not there"

M any people who have felt the sting of bullying and abuse are in retrospect grateful for the motivation it provided. Some go as far as to say the pain and suffering they experienced is one of the reasons they became successful. In truth, if we have no opposition, no conflict and no challenges we lack the compulsion to dig deep enough to discover, experience and recognise our own potential. It is the opposition that gives us an opportunity to decide who we are and what we stand for. If you never have to face a bully, you will never know that you have the power to do so. You can't climb a mountain if it is not there.

When children experience bullying, instead of focusing on the unjustness or unfairness of the situation, sit with the child and look at all the pluses, all the benefits and all the opportunities that exist as a result of someone's mean, unkind, thoughtless or cruel behaviour. If you reframe the problem long enough it does give cause for celebration. Overcoming bullying takes practice and someone has to play the bad guy.

It is clear to me now that those who have never had the benefit of rejection have also never been able to experience the joy of finding their own way, walking to the beat of their own drum and thumbing their nose at people who dismiss or dislike them. How sad to never have had the opportunity to experience the exquisite liberation that comes from being rejected and ostracised. I now wonder if it is actually a burden to go through school and high school fitting in to everyone else's expectations, feeling the need to be seen as cool and on top of things, the need to be 'in the know' and viewed as a 'together' kind of person. Is it actually draining to be constantly asking yourself what everybody else is thinking and whether you have managed to meet their standards? Is it more difficult to live with fear of rejection than actual rejection? I imagine so. What a colossal waste of precious time and energy that could be so well used creating a vivid

"Every adversity, every failure, every heartache carries with it the seed of an equal or greater benefit"

Napoleon Hill

and dynamic future, learning and creating music, art, writing, playing sport, developing ideas and new ways of thinking. Perhaps I need to write another book for all of those people who have never had the opportunity to know themselves as 'different' or 'odd' or 'quirky'. My condolences...

"Don't chase people. Be yourself, do your own thing and work hard. The right people - the ones who really belong in your life - will come to you. And stay"

Will Smith

Finding your gifts

"Most people have no idea of the giant capacity we can immediately command when we focus all of our resources on mastering a single area of our lives"

Tony Robbins

A local shopkeeper opened up to me about his experience of bullying. When he was young he was very short and skinny and was regularly bullied and teased verbally, psychologically and emotionally. He told me that he *decided* not to retaliate in anger and instead took the negative energy that he was feeling and channelled it into training hard and playing sport. He experienced a dramatic growth spurt later in high school, much to his delight, and went on to study boxing, doing very well. Through focusing his frustration and hurt into a sport he enjoyed, he found a way to excel. The self-esteem and confidence he found meant that the bullying no longer bothered him. He had not succumbed to negativity and was able to turn the rejection he experienced at school into an opportunity for his own growth and development.

He mentioned to me the often overlooked fact that many boxers are extremely peaceful people outside the ring, as they express and discharge their anger in their training and fitness programme.

Some parents choose to put their children into martial arts or self-defence classes as a strategy against bullying. This may have a positive result and it may have no impact whatsoever, depending on the child. Just as not all children are artists or musicians, not all are sporty or physically proficient. If you are teaching your child to fight so they are able to combat bullies, you may find yourself disappointed. Building skills does lead to happier and more fulfilled lives but if the skill is in an area that is of little or no interest, it is unlikely that they will put in the necessary effort to achieve a high level of success. Better to put your child into an activity that is in line with their passions.

In the schoolyard, workplace or home, it can be really difficult to see

"Give way in anything that doesn't matter, never in something that does"

Eugene Halliday

bullying as being beneficial. It is also difficult to see how focusing on your dance class, or soccer, swimming, theatre, reading, personal development, new career path, gardening, singing, school studies, computer skills etc. can make any difference to your life or have an impact on self-esteem.

When you plant a seed, for weeks and weeks it is as if you haven't done anything at all. Even so, you keep watering your seed, knowing that even this small act matters. Eventually a tiny speck appears, then a small shoot which over time grows into a tiny plant. This small plant grows and grows until eventually it becomes a tall and powerful tree. Maybe it will become the very same tree that will provide sanctuary to someone in need of a quiet space to sit and contemplate or read a good book. All this because you planted, watered and nurtured a single seed.

So it is with confidence and self-esteem. Finding an activity, course, sport, hobby etc. and developing skills, expertise, abilities and knowledge brings a myriad of benefits, not the least of which is a stronger and more vibrant sense of self and increased levels of confidence and self-esteem.

The pleasure and satisfaction you get from your achievement can be enough to help you shift the need for approval. This sense of accomplishment can be the determining factor on the journey to confidence and self-esteem. Feeling good about yourself minimises the

> *"It always seems impossible until it's done"*
>
> Nelson Mandela

unreasonable importance you may have placed on other people's opinion of you. Once you have developed your skill to a level where you are happy, where you feel increased satisfaction and pride in yourself, no one can diminish your achievement and importantly, no one can take the experience away from you.

Building up skills and knowledge may not be the answer to all your prayers, nor give you superpowers, but it goes a long way towards helping you find a new path and a healthier and more empowered mindset.

Do as the wise shopkeeper advised and to keep your head down, take the feelings of anger, sadness, frustration etc. and channel them into something that will be of benefit to you. The energy that you are feeling is valuable, powerful and creative. Focusing on the bullying and the conflict stops you from growing and developing yourself and wastes all that marvellous drive on someone who does not deserve your attention. If you turn your attention to a sport, pastime or activity that builds skill and develops you as a person, you will ultimately end up the richer for it.

The following seven-step process based on Mahatma Gandhi's teachings of non-violent resistance has been created to bring the information in this book into a succinct and easy to follow format. Here we will revisit some of the concepts and bring them together as a step by step guide to overcoming bullying, intimidation and abuse.

> *"It is not the mountain we conquer but ourselves"*
>
> Edmund Hillary

This process, along with the tools and techniques section which follows, will help you discover ways out of your problems and into solutions. This journey will take you from victim to victor, *from Bullied to Brilliant* and beyond.

"Give God time"

The Quran

SECTION 5

SEVEN STEPS TO PEACEFUL PERSONAL POWER

B-GANDHI

1. **B**reak the Pattern   Step off the tracks
2. **G**et Smart   Analyse the situation
3. **A**ssociate with like minds   Find your place or herd
4. **N**ew Systems   Make a plan
5. **D**iscover Your Why   What lights you up?
6. **H**eart   Take action and be brave
7. **I**magine   What next?

Break the Pattern
- Step off the tracks

*"Strength does not come from physical capacity.
It comes from an indomitable will"*

Mahatma Gandhi

The first step in ending the bully/victim cycle is to break the pattern of bullying and abuse and get out of the way.

The bully only has power when you are directly in their line of fire or *believe* yourself to be. Beliefs are very powerful and persuasive drivers which determine how we perceive the world around us and subsequently, our problems. Fortunately, our beliefs can and regularly do change.

If you were on a train track and saw an oncoming train, would you stand on the tracks and try to slow it down? Would you wave at it, plead with it or ask it nicely to stop? No, you would get out of the way quickly to prevent being injured or hurt. Likewise, if you are confronted by an intimidating, threatening or bullying person, perhaps rather than trying to convince them not to bully you, remove yourself from their path to a more protected location and figure out a good plan.

You may well be thinking that it is not your fault, that you didn't provoke or ask for the attention of the bully, that all this is very unfair and you shouldn't be going through this.

*"When you complain your make
yourself a victim.
Leave the situation, change the
situation or accept it.
All else is madness"*

Eckhart Tolle

The majority of the time bullies appear to seek out and target people at random. Perhaps sometimes they are testing out the water to see if they can get a bite. We know that bullies tend to target people who are calmer and gentler than the bully and unlikely to react or retaliate. They are frequently seeking relief from their circumstances through interaction with others, and causing pain to other people can bring them a momentary distraction from their own sorry and often very sad self. However, it does neither of you any good for you to become a metaphorical or physical punching bag and you have a choice as to whether you are going to be the person that offers temporary relief to the bully or not.

There are many subtle ways you can avoid placing yourself in the sights of a rampaging bully with a bad attitude. I suggest you explore all possible avenues that keep you safe or at least out of arm's length if physical violence is involved.

"Insanity is doing the same thing over and over again and expecting different results"

Albert Einstein

When I lived in Africa it became impossible for me to walk around alone even during the day. I drove everywhere, parked near the places I needed to go and was rarely alone. I was too vulnerable to attack as the colour of my skin earmarked me as a target. If you know yourself to be in danger or in the sights of a bully, then change your habits. Do not frequent areas you know the bully to be, do not put yourself into risky situations, take precautions where possible and do not open yourself up to attack.

When the bully is a family member or close friend, it is common for people to attempt to reason with them or appeal to their better nature. After all, they love you and don't really want to hurt you, do they? Think of it like this: if, from where you were standing, you believed the train to be travelling way too fast, if you thought that the train would be better off if slowed or even stopped and so that would be in a position to see things from your standpoint, would you still remain on the tracks?

Do you think the train will actually stop just because you are standing in the way and are a *nice* person, or do you think you would be safer for you if you stepped to the side? If you were determined to get your message across to the train, could you not, from safety, call out, wave a flag or gesture with your arms?

When you are faced with an antagonist of any sort and feeling intimidated, is it a good idea to stand right in front of them, to be in their direct line of fire, negotiate, discuss or debate the problem? Or would it help if you were somewhat to the side, out of harm's reach? If your desire is to remain in a relationship with this person, as in a family situation, would this be easier to achieve when you are not feeling threatened or afraid?

The same applies if you are dealing with a bully that is emotionally or physically intent on engaging you in their drama and likely to cause you harm. Get off the tracks, out of the way and wait somewhere safe until the crisis is over.

"Why do bullies bully? Because they can!"

A great number of people are bullied in their own homes and so the possibility of creating physical distance becomes a critical issue. Ultimately the decision of how willing you are to allow that person to operate in your space and what behaviours are acceptable depends greatly on your own vision of the world and your ability to set up *non-negotiable* boundaries. Therein lies the answer to the real bully/victim cycle. Self-confidence, a willingness to take action and the ability to be clear about personal boundaries is a powerful formula for healing and/or ending toxic relationships.

If however the bully is outside the home, it is far easier to take steps that will reduce or even eliminate contact with that person. If the problem is at school, make sure you are sitting as far away from the bully as possible. Involve your teacher and parents or carers in this process. Avoid arriving at or leaving the classroom at the same time when possible. If there are problems on the school bus then make other arrangements for travel or sit close to the driver.

Under no circumstances is physical violence acceptable at home or in the schoolyard. Physical intimidation is the lowest operating mode of human behaviour and at no point does it bring any value or growth to any relationship.

If the bullying becomes physical or violent then it is immediately the responsibility of responsible adults to take control and intervene. No person should live in fear of physical violence and it is the absolute legal right of every student to attend school without fearing for their physical safety. We all have the power and potential to overcome all other forms of bullying regardless of the intensity or ugliness; however there are times when it is better to move on from the school/job/relationship and find better battles.

If you choose to stay in a situation, self-confidence, a willingness to take action and the ability to be clear about personal boundaries are required if you are going to effectively resolve the problem. When it is a school issue, the child depends at this point entirely on the adults to provide a safe physical environment. It is up to the parents or carers and the school to ensure the safety and physical well-being of the child. It is up to the child (in conjunction with the school authorities and their parents or carers) to develop the necessary strategies to overcome emotional and psychological intimidation.

Bullies bully, that is what they do. The real question is, who is paying attention? Abandon your feelings about the unfairness of this situation. It does not serve you to be resentful and does not help or improve your circumstance in any way. Like it or not, life presents us continuously with perfect opportunities for learning and growth and these opportunities often look like and feel like disasters.

"If you really want to be happy, nobody can stop you"

Sister Mary Tricky

The question is not whether it is fair that you are being bullied (blame and victimhood), the question is what do you need to learn so that you don't have to experience this again (personal power and resourcefulness).

Action taken out of fear or anger will *not* bring you long-term relief and in general will bring no relief at all. Be certain that *all* steps come from a love of self and others so that once your problem has been resolved you find yourself back in balance, filled with new learnings and empowered. Live life so that when you play the re-run through your mind, you can enjoy it for a second time. Anger and retribution have a bitter taste to them and do not bring any comfort.

If stepping away from bullying or abuse causes you to find yourself without friends or family support, it is important to make decisions based on your well-being and not out of fear of being alone. There are times in life when we find ourselves faced with change and in these periods we can often find ourselves seemingly without an adequate network. Trust in your own resourcefulness and your ability to create a new and more peaceful environment for yourself. Solitude in itself does not need to be seen as a negative and can at times prove to be a welcome respite. Take the opportunity of aloneness to discover more about yourself, your dreams, desires, strengths and weaknesses. The answer to your problem lies in the quietness of your mind. Take time to listen.

Understand that you are not the first person, and will definitely not be the last, to be faced with a problem like this. Many people have been bullied before you, and many will be after you. Be willing to let go of what you currently know and how you have managed things like this in the past. In doing this, by taking a step in a new direction, you are creating new ways of handling yourself and the situations you find yourself in, so that you now create a healthier, happier and more creative environment for yourself.

"There is no value in life except what you choose to place upon it and no happiness in any place except what you bring to it yourself"

Henry David Thoreau

G et Smart
– Analyse the situation

"God grant me the serenity to accept the things I cannot change, the courage to change the things I can, and the wisdom to know the difference"

Reinhold Niebuhr

In this step it is time to properly consider what is actually going on. Look more closely at the bully's circumstances and behaviour. Look at the choices they make, the friends they attract, the things they are interested in, how they see the world and importantly, the words they use to describe it. Do you honour and value the choices the bully is making, given their behaviour? Would you instinctively choose them as a friend when they are acting this way? Or is your gut impulse to reject if not them, then at the very least their behaviour?

If your impulse is or has been to reject them either through thought or action, be aware that they will inevitably already feel your rejection, either consciously or unconsciously and will be acting accordingly. Whether you have been able to keep your feelings and thoughts to yourself or not, at some level the bully will already be keenly aware that you do not respect or value their behaviour and this in itself can be enough to provoke them to attack. Feeling undervalued or unloved motivates many acts of anger or aggression and human beings are far more intuitive than they realise.

"Give us grace and strength to forbear and to persevere. Give us courage and gaiety and the quiet mind, spare to us our friends, soften to us our enemies"

Robert Louis Stevenson

Rejection by the victim is not the only cause but it is remarkably common in situations where the victim and bully are well acquainted. There can also be a multitude of reasons why hostility erupts and is justified in the eyes of the bully. If you do not have any reservations about the bully, if it is someone you barely know or don't know at all, a bully will still be able to justify aggressive or hurtful behaviour towards you based on their view of the world and the feelings they have when they are around you.

They may decide they don't like the way you look, the way you dress, the colour of your skin, your race, religious beliefs, sexual preference, weight, height, gender or any number of equally unreasonable prejudices. Another trigger for conflict can be if you remind the bully of someone who they have bad feelings towards. If the bullying occurs in a bar or club and alcohol is involved, it can be the result of simple misunderstandings and is instigated by a person who has lost control of themselves. Sadly we have seen many serious and even fatal incidences of 'coward punches' where this has been the case.

At this point it may be extremely difficult to consider the bully with anything but antagonism or hatred. It is easy to vilify and condemn the bully as an evil and despicable person who deserves misfortune and punishment, but it is also narrow-minded and one-sided. Hopefully by now we have learned that there are no simple cases of bullying, nor are there simple answers to ridding our world of the presence of bullies.

The reality is that our world is home to some fairly damaged and hostile individuals who have grown up under difficult and sometimes unbearable circumstances. Our job is to teach ourselves and our children how to recognise and manage the consequences of these people showing up in our lives.

"Hate the sin, love the sinner"

Mahatma Gandhi

When considering a bully, first consider their origins and influences. Consider how they have come to the conclusions they have reached and perhaps why they have chosen a path filled with conflict and difficulty over a more peaceful and loving existence.

It may be uncomfortable, especially if you are feeling hurt, but take some time to imagine what this situation looks like through the eyes of the bully. How do they see the world and what kind of story do they have? Do they feel loved and supported? Do they have a warm and loving home environment or life history? Do they experience real joy on a regular basis? Are they generally peaceful and kind and sensitive to others? What influences are present in their life that have caused them to choose a path of hostility and conflict?

"The key to overcoming bullying is to see it as an opportunity; the lesson is in the learnings. To end the cycle, focus on what needs to be learned and what needs to be done"

You can be assured that if someone is bullying they are not in a state of inner bliss, serenity and happiness. Something is definitely off track for them.

There is also a strong chance that they don't even realise this to be true and would feel even more hostile towards you were you to point it out.

This does not mean you need to take responsibility for helping them. You may be the very last person on the planet that can do them any good at all. What you can do is recognise that bullies bully for a reason and that reason is ultimately as a result of choices they have made throughout their lifetime, whether they be child or adult.

It must be hard living the life of a bully. Ultimately all bullies lose. If you are able to see them as a person who is in pain, you may find it easier to forgive them. If you find it too hard to forgive the person, forgive the person they would have been if they had grown up in different circumstances. Forgive the person they would have been if they were happy. You can however, rest assured that the reason they are bullying is *not* a reflection of your value and worth. They are bullying because somewhere inside, they are hurting.

Ultimately, *why* the bully is bullying is irrelevant unless you have some authority over them or have received an invitation from them to help, both of which are unlikely. Otherwise, once you have noticed that the bully is a bully, start looking at what you can do to turn the situation around.

Let go of the need to be right. Remember to pay attention to the reality the bully is faced with. Is this problem as straightforward as it seems? Of all the options that surround you, can you imagine that there is something more available to you right now that does not come laced with the toxic emotions of anger, sadness, fear, hurt, guilt or grief? Are there ways of seeing this situation that propel you on to better things, that lift you up instead of crushing you down, that heal your heart instead of torturing it, that bring you back to your joy instead of dragging you into the dark abyss of negative emotions?

"Love and compassion are necessities, not luxuries. Without them humanity cannot survive"

Dalai Lama

Know that if you are in emotional pain, you are simply lacking information. Many other people have found themselves in as much pain and confusion as you and yet found ways of returning to their joy and their passion. If it is possible for them, it is possible for you.

Ask yourself, what is there to learn that will take the emotion, the pain and the energy out of this problem? Examine everything you currently have at your disposal and be objective about what has happened or is happening. Imagine you are looking through the eyes of your closest friend or a mentor and seeing the problem from their point of view. What would they say to you? What advice would they give?

"You can't wake a person who is pretending to be asleep"

Navajo Proverb

Consider what this problem will look like one year or five years from now, if you do something about it. Consider also what it will look like if you don't. See the bigger picture, understand how this situation will bring you growth and look outside of the box for your solutions.

Sadly, many people find themselves in the position of being bullied. Happily, many of them find a way through and a way out of the bullying situation. And if they can, you can too. Consider what you may have failed to notice up until now that could change everything, or at least something, for the better. Questions such as this will help you find insight within yourself to improve your situation and create a healthier, happier and more creative environment for yourself and those you love.

"If we could read the secret history of our enemies we should find in each man's life sorrow and suffering enough to disarm all hostility"

Henry Wadsworth Longfellow

Associate with Like Minds
- Find your place or herd

"The world is a dangerous place to live; not because of the people who are evil, but because of the people who don't do anything about it"

Albert Einstein

Originally human beings were tribal. We were born, raised and died amongst a close knit clan of family and clan members. We were educated, challenged and protected by the people around us. If there was a threat to our safety, the tribe would be there for us and we would be there for the tribe. Modern day living, with its fractured and destabilised family units, leaves many people feeling isolated and lacking in support.

We need to empower children with strategies and tools to handle difficult situations and share with them the importance of creating a sense of tribal allegiance.

The school environment is isolating for many children. It is only since the Industrial Revolution that children have been required to remain together in large numbers, enclosed in a defined area with many opportunities to avoid supervision and be expected to get along. The majority of schools do their best to instil a sense of tribal philosophy, tradition, and social expectation but even so, there are children who feel themselves to be outsiders, lacking in community and connection.

"We can live without religion and meditation, but we cannot survive without human affection"

Dalai Lama

It is our job to create a sense of identity, help them to form allegiance to their school beyond the uniform and the colours and understand their emotional responsibility to each other. They need to see their school and their peers as family and for that to happen, they need to feel loved.

There is great power in numbers. All significant changes to our world have come about when a small group of individuals have inspired others to join with them and effect that change. Team building, relationship building and goal setting for schools and workplaces is not only essential, it needs to be a priority. We need to recognise and energise the communities and sub-groups that exist already in our environs and encourage them to support each other. Most importantly, we need to remember how to demonstrate *love* and be brave enough to use that word out loud in any situation.

Ask a classroom of students to talk about the latest crime show or action movie and you will have hours of talk time. Ask them to discuss different ways they can demonstrate love for each other and you will have to dig deep to get a reasonable and authentic response. Paradoxically, it is not our connection with violence that will see us out of this situation, it is our connection and understanding of the true meaning of love.

Love is a powerful friend and ally. Love binds us together in the face of problems, love carries us through trauma, grief and heartache and love heals all wounds.

"Don't walk behind me; I may not lead. Don't walk in front of me; I may not follow. Just walk beside me and be my friend"

Albert Camus

Wild animals are smart; they use what they have to hand to protect each other. As supposedly the most intelligent species on the planet, why aren't we doing the same?

Animals when faced with danger gather in a circle facing the predator, often surrounding their young and protecting the old or infirm. They create a huddle against a lethal and terrifying predator. We are no different. In the face of a threatening or challenging situation, including terrorism and war, the most influential tool at humanity's disposal is and always has been the sheer power of numbers.

Some time ago a friend of mine experienced some minor cyber bullying. She was openly attacked and belittled through social media by a higher-profiled business woman. It was interesting to see the amount of people who were willing to jump to her defence. She had an impressive online huddle happening in a matter of hours which quickly defused the situation. I imagine it also gave her a real boost to know that so many people were concerned and keen to support her. There was great power in that moment.

Imagine if we did that for each other all the time. Perhaps students could be encouraged to take action if the situation permitted. They could learn that if they notice bullying or intimidation in any shape or form, they could stop what they are doing and stand near to the child who is having difficulty and raise their hand. It would not be necessary to say or do anything at all. All they would need to do would be to stand near to the person who was in distress. Imagine two or four or even ten or twenty or so children walking over to the person who is feeling upset and under attack and simply standing with them, hands raised in silence, looking at the perpetrator. No blame, no anger, no defensiveness. Standing, still, together. Instead of being a bystander you could be *standing by*, offering support and ready to help in any way you can.

A great difficulty present in many schoolyard situations is that the bystanders feel nervous and uncertain about what they need to do. Standing near to someone who is feeling a little isolated or alone could be literally and figuratively a step in the right direction.

> *"Whenever you are confronted with an opponent, conquer him with love"*
>
> Mahatma Gandhi

Imagine if we accepted that as a given for all human beings. That our unspoken code encouraged bystanders, if their personal security was not at risk, to make their way over to the people involved without comment or physical act, without condemnation or criticism, without defensiveness or attack, using sheer numbers to defuse tensions.

Unfortunately it is often not the case that when you are bullied or intimidated you suddenly find yourself surrounded by supportive friends. In fact more often than not it is quite the opposite. A great deal of bullying occurs out of eyesight or earshot of potential witnesses or is carried out surreptitiously through the use of technology. If this is the case for you or your child right now, effort and determination is required to alert and mobilise potential bystanders or supporters.

To complicate matters further, the victim will sometimes hide the fact that they are feeling bullied, out of shame. They feel ashamed of being targeted, worried they are somehow defective or deficient, so don't tell others that they are hurting. They then go on to feel even worse because nobody notices that they are in pain. The unwillingness of the victim to speak up and seek help allows the problem to persist and grow to unacceptable levels. This is a destructive and damaging response to bullying and one that needs to be caught as early as possible.

There are several helplines and organisations listed in the resources section of this book and you can find many more specific to your country or area online.

Don't mistake the feeling of being alone as being true in and of itself. There are *always* people and resources in our environment that can help and support you when you are in need. If you can't see them right now, it is simply that you haven't pointed your attention in the right direction, asked the right person or rung the right number. Look, investigate and discover what lies hidden from view right now that could change your situation completely. There is someone ready, willing and able to help and support you right now. Make sure you find them.

*"Do what you can,
with what you have, where you are"*

Theodore Roosevelt

New Systems
– Make a plan

"I have no special talent. I am only passionately curious"

Albert Einstein

Let's do a quick recap. You have by now successfully moved out of the way of the bully or, at the very least, managed to minimise the negative impact they are having on your life. You have had time to consider your circumstances, you have carefully analysed the situation and looked at the problem from many angles including through the bully's eyes. You have looked at the people and resources that surround you and have a greater understanding of the situation you have found yourself in and what you can do to change it. You have found a really great tree, quiet place, haven or sanctuary. You have understood the need to find peace in solitude. Now you are ready to make a plan.

If Alice continues to travel without a direction or purpose, she may well find herself back in exactly the same place she started. When you are emerging out of a pattern of bullying, it is wise to choose a new course that leads you to a different experience.

"Would you tell me, please, which way I ought to go from here?". "That depends a good deal on where you want to get to," said the Cat. "I don't much care where--" said Alice. "Then it doesn't matter which way you go," said the Cat"

(Alice's Adventures in Wonderland) – Lewis Carroll

It is time to create a workable plan that will give you freedom from repeating or re-energising the bullying pattern that you have been sitting in, and focus your attention elsewhere. It is time to decide what you want to do with all the fabulous free time you have just created. As you have now decided to no longer focus on bullies and conflict, you are free to do whatever you choose. It's rather liberating, actually. No matter what age you are, setting and creating goals and objectives makes life purposeful and interesting. If you are not driving your life then your life will be driving you. In order to get exactly what you want you have to *focus* on exactly what you want. If you are going to set your internal GPS and make a decision to move in the direction of your dreams, you will need clarity about what you want.

Goal setting and visioning are important in relation to overcoming bullying, as one of the natural outcomes of confidence and self-esteem building is a renewed interest in life opportunities that present. We all need something to hope for, something to dream of and something to achieve. It is how we move away from purely survival-based living and is an important aspect of growth and development. When coaching people who feel stuck or apathetic about life, the coach will always shift attention onto a goal or activity that feels inspiring, motivating and energised. Humans, both young and old, need purpose in their lives. It is a way out of sadness and depression and valuable when developing successful long-term life strategies.

> *"All our dreams can come true, if we have the courage to pursue them"*
>
> Walt Disney

> *"When you lose, don't lose the lesson"*
>
> Dalai Lama

The Dalai Lama is the spiritual and temporal leader of the Tibetan people. In 1989 His Holiness was awarded the Nobel Peace Prize for his non-violent struggle for the liberation of Tibet. Since 1959 he has been living in exile in India, and Tibet continues to be occupied by communist China. He has indeed more reason than most to fall into rage, bitterness and despair at his life experience and the treatment of his people. The Dalai Lama, bless him, has a completely different view.

Although he was born into his leadership role, the Dalai Lama has successfully created a worldwide following of Buddhists and non-Buddhists alike because of his dedicated and unswerving approach to his life's work through study, meditation, and a great willingness to share his learning on a global scale. Despite the extraordinary difficulties he has had to face, he is a man who exudes a remarkable degree of happiness, mischievousness and joyful inner bliss. He has achieved this through peaceful means by stepping away from the bullying, remaining true to his spiritual beliefs and practices, and advocating against retribution, violence or conflict as a solution.

He demonstrates that in order to follow goals, dreams and aspirations and to build a compelling picture of who you are and what you represent, you need to take *consistent*, focused and disciplined action regardless of who stands in your way.

Given most of us do not face nearly the same level of bullying and intimidation as the Dalai Lama, applying these same principles to achieving our own dreams and aspirations should be simple. Step away from the bullying, make a plan and then take action. If you wish to be a singer, then take singing lessons, read books about other singers, go to performances, join performance groups and go to auditions. If you wish to be a gardener then read about plants and gardening, meet other gardeners, establish a garden and get out there. If you wish to be an accountant, then study accounting, meet other accountants and take action towards your goal. If you wish to travel, then research travel destinations, talk to people who have travelled and find a way to realise your dream. It is not money or opportunity that holds us back from our dreams, it is fear, inertia and an unwillingness to act.

> "If one advances confidently in the direction of his dreams, and endeavours to live the life which he has imagined, he will meet with success unexpected in common hours"
>
> Henry David Thoreau

Once you have decided on a plan it is important to write it down. Writing things down is a necessary and powerful link between thought and action and essential to the creative process. It brings dreams into form and makes manifest your mind. Writing down goals and dreams powerfully enhances the process of turning thought into physical reality.

For this process, it helps to have a diary or notebook that is specifically used for goal setting and planning. When you go to sleep put it near your bed so if you wake in the night with inspiration you can quickly jot down your thoughts before you forget.

Write a comprehensive list of goals. Be as specific as you can and write them in the *present tense* as if you had already achieved your goal, e.g. 'I now have…' or 'I now am…' or 'I now can…' and then mark next to your goal the date when you feel you can achieve that goal. This serves to 'programme' your unconscious mind and will dramatically expedite the realisation of your goal. For example: *'I have now passed all my exams and successfully graduated from school – 15 Dec'* or *'I now can play three songs on my guitar—1 Sept'*. It is important you write the specific year you wish to achieve your goal along with the date.

Once you have decided on your short, medium and long-term goals, write down the steps you need to take to move towards those goals. For instance: *'I am now fit, flexible and exercising three times a week – 30 Aug 20--*. The steps I need to take are:

> The definition of happiness: "The full use of your powers along lines of excellence"
>
> John F. Kennedy

- ❀ Stretch every morning for 15 minutes
- ❀ Run every morning for 15 minutes
- ❀ Enrol at the local gym.

Discover Your Why
– *What lights you up?*

"He who has a why to live can bear almost any how"

Friedrich Nietzsche

Once you have clarity about what you want, you then need to focus on *why* you want these things. The *why* is where the power lies. Why you do what you do is the inspiration that will get you out of bed each morning with a spring in your step and push you to move towards your plans, goals or dreams. Your *why* is your creative power source.

Discovering your *why* is a little bit trickier than goal setting, as we are mostly unconscious of what drives us. Some people are very clear about why they do what they do but on the whole, if you ask people what they want or why they want it, they are at a loss. Inevitably, the people who get what they want in life have generally been very clear about what they wanted and why they wanted it.

Your *why* could be because you want wealth, fame or adoration. It could be that you would like a particular car, or a nice house. Some people have more altruistic or simple desires and would like to be able to help others, be surrounded by family, be comfortable, be safe or stable. Others are more driven by the need for freedom, to be without ties or limitations and so choose careers or family situations that allow them to be nomadic, fluid and spontaneous. Whether you are aware of it or not, there is always a compelling *why* that guides your decision-making processes and ultimately directs your life choices. If you take the time to consider and understand your *why,* you will have a clear indication of how and why your life looks as it does today.

The desire for money itself does not generally hold enough of an energetic pull to galvanise most human beings into action unless there is a compelling *why* to back it up. This accounts for our societal obsession with the lottery. Most of us prefer to dream and imagine an abundance of wealth falling into our laps rather than taking action in the

"The grand essentials of happiness are: something to do, something to love, and something to hope for"

Allan K. Chalmers

often difficult and laborious task of applying ourselves to our chosen profession, passion or purpose and generating wealth for ourselves.

Many people are driven by negative influencers and often self-made billionaires have rags to riches tales. They have successfully used the fear of poverty to drive them to dizzying financial successes. The negative *why,* however, comes with a catch. If your *why* is moving away from poverty, then when you achieve financial success, you will lose your motivation. You would then need to examine your driving influences and make changes to give you a new motivator. If you don't you may well lose everything you have earned.

> *"We must accept finite disappointment, but we must never lose infinite hope"*
>
> Martin Luther King

The desire to provide an abundant and loving home for your family, for artistic expression, or the need for freedom and travel can be highly motivating *whys* and inspire enough incentive to do what it takes to get a result.

Discovering and focusing on your positive *why* is one of the most powerfully profound and life transforming practices on the path to personal growth and development. Your *why* is your reason for doing what you do; your *why* is your connection to inspiration and creativity. Your *why* gives meaning and direction to everything you do. Your *why* is your purpose, the expression of your unique set of talents and gifts.

When you discover your *why* you recognise your deeper self and connect to your personal and ever-present source of unlimited and unbridled joie de vivre. Your *why* is your own inbuilt 'on switch' which is currently silently flashing away inside you, awaiting your push. Ask Sir Richard Branson what gets him out of bed in the morning and he will not say it is the desire for more money. The love of his family is clearly one of the major drivers in his life. Having difficulty at school and struggling with dyslexia also may have formed strong motivations to achieve and succeed. The desire to prove others wrong can be a powerful driver. We should however, never underestimate the power of love.

> *"I cannot remember a moment in my life when I have not felt the love of my family"*
>
> Richard Branson

An example of someone who is intimately acquainted with his *why,* aligned with his purpose and is a modern day beacon of light is the 14th Dalai Lama:

"As long as there is a lack of the inner discipline that brings calmness of mind, no matter what external facilities or conditions you have, they will never give you the feeling of joy and happiness

that you are seeking. On the other hand, if you possess this inner quality, a calmness of mind, a degree of stability within, then even if you lack various external facilities that you would normally consider necessary for happiness, it is still possible to live a happy and joyful life."

He has shown us, as have all great spiritual masters, that how you see or perceive your circumstances *determines* your experience. That having a clear understanding of your purpose for being on this planet gives access to a powerful resourcefulness and the ability to transform even the most tragic of situations into knowledge, wisdom and learning.

So often we can forget that we have the power to create lives that are not only worth living, but that we love living. It is not money or opportunity that holds us back from our dreams. It is fear, inertia and an unwillingness to take action. When you know what lights you up, and you frequently and regularly spend time in the places, with the people and in the spaces that light you up you create a healthier, happier and more creative environment for yourself and those you love.

"The best and most beautiful things in the world cannot be seen or even touched. They must be felt with the heart"

Helen Keller

H eart
– *Take action and be brave*

"Most important, have the courage to follow your heart and intuition. They somehow already know what you truly want to become"

Steve Jobs

No great achievement has ever come from playing it safe. The most challenging aspect of any plan is stepping up and putting it into action. The planning, strategising, developing, understanding and imagining phase can be exciting and absorbing, so much so that some people spend their lives dreaming and planning a better life. If it is not followed up with action, your dream will remain forever a dream. The courage to step forward, and importantly the courage to believe in yourself are key components on your journey to the future you dream of. No good ever came from simply wishing things were different.

The process of overcoming bullying is fundamentally a journey of courage. You need the courage to look at things differently, the courage to move away from what you are used to and most importantly, the courage to do what is right.

Many of us are relatively happy, living lives of quiet and dull desperation waiting for the right time to come along so that we can make changes or worse, waiting for a surprise windfall or random piece of good fortune to befall us. Unfortunately, all big decisions are made with insufficient information and the right time is just an illusion. You are never ready, the timing is never perfect and you will never feel absolutely certain about your outcome.

If you have the courage to act, what you will know is that you are doing something, moving towards

"Life is the art of drawing sufficient conclusions from insufficient premises"

Samuel Butler

your goals and no matter how minutely, making progress. You can't start a movement if you don't move. You will, at the very least, know that you are living.

How do we know we are doing the right thing? Well, we don't. Certainty is for the faint hearted. Life is ultimately a climb and we can't always see the top, or even where we are in relation to the mountain. Courage, confidence and trust are essential if we are to make significant changes in our lives.

> *"Life is change. Growth is optional. Choose wisely"*
>
> Karen Kaiser Clark

Teaching ourselves or our children to tune in to our intuition or gut feeling is essential. Equally important is developing a sense of certainty and self-belief as a result. If we do not know and trust our own internal guidance system, whose guidance are can we rely on?

People who have been bullied often experience a big knock in their confidence. The good news is that you can recover your confidence—it comes from self-belief, the ability to trust your own instincts, intuitions or gut feeling even when faced with opposition, and the courage to step up and do what is necessary. When you recover your confidence you also create a healthier, happier and more creative environment for yourself and those you love.

> *"Happiness is when what you think, what you say, and what you do are in harmony"*
>
> Mahatma Gandhi

Imagine
– What next?

"Imagination is more important than knowledge"

Albert Einstein

Now you have set your goals, taken action and are moving in the right direction, it's time to spread your wings and fly a little higher.

All human endeavour originates in imagination. It's time to use the new momentum you have created to springboard you into a more resourceful and fulfilled life. Take all the painful experiences you have already had and bring value to all you have learned to propel you towards new and better things. Use your pain for your benefit, for your growth and development. Use it wisely, with intention and with gratitude. Let your imagination be your guide and create something valuable, something that serves both you and others and causes you to never, ever look back.

One of the characteristics that differentiates many notable people in history is their ability to dream a bigger dream and importantly, their ability to take the pain of their past and transform it into learnings. One thing you can be sure of, in the top 500 historically renowned people, an extremely high percentage will have overcome remarkable difficulties to achieve what they have achieved and 100% will have at some time experienced deep pain.

"In 20 years' time you will have more regrets about the things you didn't do than the things you did"

Mark Twain

You have now and will always have the ability to change your circumstances, learn new skills, change your mind and take steps towards the life you dream of. The one thing you have complete control of is your interpretation of your life and the conclusions you draw from it. It is not what happens to you in life that defines you; it is the choices you make as a consequence.

If everything you have experienced up until this moment in time were bundled together as a powerful and transformational education in life skills, you would be able to make much better decisions about your future. Imagine if you could take your learning and reach for the potential that lies inside you right now, waiting to be called forth. Would you spread your wings and fly?

"In a gentle way, you can shake the world"

Mohandas Gandhi

Abou Ben Adhem

Abou Ben Adhem (may his tribe increase!)
Awoke one night from a deep dream of peace,
And saw, within the moonlight in his room,
Making it rich, and like a lily in bloom,
An angel writing in a book of gold:

Exceeding peace had made Ben Adhem bold,
And to the presence in the room he said,
"What writest thou?" The vision raised its head,
And with a look made of all sweet accord
Answered, "The names of those who love the Lord."

"And is mine one?" said Abou. "Nay, not so,"
Replied the angel. Abou spoke more low,
But cheerily still; and said, "I pray thee, then,
Write me as one who loves his fellow men."

The angel wrote, and vanished. The next night
It came again with a great wakening light,
And showed the names whom love of God had blessed,
And, lo! Ben Adhem's name led all the rest!

James Henry Leigh Hunt
1784-1859

SECTION 6

TOOLS AND TECHNIQUES

"Freedom is always and exclusively the freedom for the one who thinks differently"

Rosa Luxemburg

Unfortunately, and this is the bad news, try as you might, there is no way you can absolutely predict or pre-empt the behaviour of others. Likewise, controlling and managing the behaviour of others is not your domain, nor is it for you to judge, cajole, coerce, manipulate or force people to do the 'right thing' as you see it. If you were able to do these things, you would be imposing on another's free will and that could make you a bully.

What we can control is how regularly (if at all) we put ourselves in front of people who hurt us. We can choose whether we wish to either oppose them or remove ourselves from the situation.

Your state of mind and your physical location are actually all you have control over. What you think and feel when the person is attacking or attempting to hurt you and how long you are going to hang around and put up with their hostility needs to be your primary concern. How far do you want it to go? What do you hope to achieve by staying and have you factored in your physical safety?

Bullying has many forms and appears in many fields. Just as we would like the bully to recognise the role they play and the impact they have on the people around them, if you experience bullying regularly then it is time to recognise that the common denominator is actually you. If you have found yourself regularly in conflict with bullies, be aware that this is *your* problem and as a result you must take steps towards achieving a different outcome.

A bully wants their own way and will often push as hard as they can to get it. If they are deeply entrenched in the dominance pattern, as most bullies are, they will only remain interested in you as long as they believe themselves able to dominate.

There are many emotions and sensations that accompany the experience of being bullied, and they can be all the more acute when the bullying comes from within a family or from a close friend. Physical reactions can include nausea, trembling, dizziness, breathlessness, heart palpitations, over-eating, under-eating, exhaustion and other stress-related responses.

"Do what you can, with what you have, where you are"

Theodore Roosevelt

When you find yourself being attacked, ostracised, abandoned or bullied it is common to experience symptoms such as shame, guilt, fear, sadness, humiliation and loss of confidence. You may buy into their story of who you are and see yourself as worthless or less-than, and at worst you may experience depression, hopelessness and despair.

A common response to bullying is to buy into what the bully is saying and question your own value and worth. It is all too easy to torture yourself by trying to understand their thinking and unravel the threads that lead them to think so badly of you. It is common for the victim to wrangle with the picture that has been presented and struggle to fathom how the bully has come to such awful conclusions. On the whole we find it easier to believe someone who is saying dreadful things about us than to take and believe any compliments we receive. Many of us are taught as children to be self-deprecating and that it is good manners to reject compliments. This is flawed thinking and one of the reasons bullying is so effective.

"No man ever got very high by pulling other people down. The intelligent merchant does not knock his competitors. The sensible worker does not knock those who work with him. Don't knock your friends. Don't knock your enemies. Don't knock yourself"

Alfred Lord Tennyson

Your focus when faced with bullying or those who wish to demean, slander, ostracise or belittle you needs to be how you respond emotionally, mentally and physically to what they are saying. Do not allow yourself to agree with the bully. Make a conscious decision to ensure your well-being is your focus next time you find yourself confronted with hostility.

When you find yourself under attack or feeling threatened, notice how your body is responding. Your heart may race and you may temporarily feel disorientated, dizzy or nauseous. Being attacked or threatened by someone you love and care about puts the phrase 'You make me sick' in a whole different light.

Over time, you can develop a system to cope with the initial intimidation or bullying attack. Although being attacked is never pleasant and the initial sting may still be a bit of a shock, it is possible to learn how to easily and rapidly step through the process of coping with bullying and move on to more healthy and life enhancing practices. Practise makes perfect, so they say, and the very bullying that is intended to hurt you and bring you down, can afford you the resources and tools to overcome it.

"Nobody can hurt me without my permission"

Mohandas Gandhi

What To Say To Your Kids When Things Go Wrong

"The strength of a nation derives from the integrity of the home"

Confucius

When children come home from school feeling rejected by their peers, it is natural for parents to fall into a state of worry and stress. They may wonder if there something *wrong* with their child. They may question whether their child is to blame, whether there is a larger problem to investigate, whether the school should be informed, or if it is normal, innocent schoolyard behaviour.

The key to successfully overcoming the problem is to see the situation as a valuable learning experience and convey that effectively to the child. The lesson is in the learnings that come from the bullying situation, not from the bullying itself. Focusing on the problem only exacerbates the problem and creates a cycle of victimhood. In abusive relationships people play out either the role of aggressor or victim. The way to end the cycle is to focus on what needs to be learned and what needs to be done.

Firstly, gather as much information as possible. Sit with your child and focus solely on them while you discuss what's happening. Your child deserves your attention, as to them this problem can seem insurmountable. To adults, financial issues, global issues, family issues and health issues are all critical; to a child, playground issues are catastrophic.

- ❀ Always take the situation seriously and actively intervene early
- ❀ Encourage your child to calmly talk about it
- ❀ Get the facts: who, when, where, what
- ❀ Prepare your child how to respond internally and behaviourally
- ❀ Discuss and develop strategies to boost their self-confidence
- ❀ When necessary, involve school officials and/or police
- ❀ Follow up and keep discussion going
- ❀ Know when to seek professional help

Reframing

A valuable technique that can be used to shift thought patterns is reframing. Reframing is the process of looking far enough outside the box to see that gain and bringing it into our conscious awareness.

Ask your child:

In what way is this situation of benefit?
What can you learn from this?

Focus on the gain from the problem rather than the pain from the problem. If we allow our minds to stretch far enough, every situation can be seen as a gain.

For example:

Problem: *"My teacher is mean to me."*
Reframe: *"What a great opportunity for you to discover how to cope with difficult teachers. How great is it going to be for you to have these skills?"*

Problem: *"I hate school"*
Reframe: *"How will you learn to face the challenges of social interaction if you do not go to school? School can be confronting at times as it is the place where we learn about different personalities, learn new skills and figure out how we see ourselves in relation to the world. We find out where our strengths and weaknesses are and we learn how to function in a group. School is the stepping stone between childhood and the adult world and is intended to be a safe place for you to develop as an individual. There are many advantages to school and often there are great teachers and students to help along the way. If you are finding school difficult we should sit down and discuss what can be done to improve things for you."*

Problem: *"Everyone thinks I am ugly."*
Reframe: *"Describe beauty to me. Describe ugly to me. The words we use to describe these are unique for each of us. Everyone has a different idea of beauty and it is absolutely impossible to know what the people you meet are thinking. What is beauty to one is ugly for another. How do you know that 'everybody' thinks you are ugly? If you focus on what other people think you will never find peace nor any certainty. What if someone tells you they think you are ugly but are not being truthful? How can you know? Be grateful for what you have and put your attention into what you can do with your life, not whether or not you have the approval of others."*

"A good laugh and a long sleep are the two best cures for anything"

Irish Proverb

Bullying Discussion - *A simple guide*

When addressing the specific problem of bullying, draw out as much information as possible before forming any conclusions. When analysing the problem it is important to speak in specific terms and avoid generalisations and dramatic or sensationalised language.

The three step process is:

1. Draw out as much information as possible
2. Discuss the problem in detail and provide alternative perspectives
3. Create a plan of action.

The following questions will help to achieve this, however each child, parent and carer will have different ways of viewing problems and different interpretations of behaviour. This is to be used as a rough guide which may prompt your own questions.

What exactly is the problem?
What specifically is happening?
Who specifically is involved?
How is that a problem for you?
Is there another way of looking at this problem?
What can you learn from this situation?
How are you feeling?
What possible solutions are there?
Do you need to confront the person or can you let it go?
Are you okay?
Do you need someone to intervene or can you handle this one?
What is your plan?
Is there anything I can do to help?

Once you have a clear understanding of the problem, you can reframe. For instance:

> *"You are very lucky to be able to experience these difficulties when you are a child and have people around who love you to support you. Imagine how great it is going to feel when you have learned how to deal with this and are good at coping with someone who is (angry, hurtful, unfair, mean, aggressive, unkind, bossy etc.). This will be really useful to you when you are grown up and managing problems on your own. People like this won't be able to bother you then as you will have learned how to handle them at school.*
>
> *His job, as a bully, is to push you to the point whereby you are so uncomfortable that you have to figure out how to handle this situation without getting sad about yourself. Your job is to figure out a way of managing and coping with people like him and understanding that although not everybody is going to treat you well, you have the tools and resources you need to overcome these kind of problems.*
>
> *Find a way to get around the bully. Find a way of keeping out of his way and having a better experience at school but most of all, find a way to not take his behaviour personally. You see him as being unkind and cruel, that is his story, not yours. His unkindness comes from within his heart for whatever reason and he may or may not one day understand this. Don't take it on."*

When discussing the problem with your child, the words you use are very important. Your role is to extract as real a picture as possible so you are able to talk about what is actually going on, as opposed to what your child *thinks* is going on. Perspective is the key. A great deal of bullying is psychological, so your child already has all the tools and resources inside them to overcome the problem.

These are simply guidelines and you need to develop your own set of specific questions and create reframes that are in line with your child's thinking.

Ask questions that encourage your child to examine their thinking and recognise the opportunities or gaps in thinking that exist. For instance:

Child: *"I hate school. Nobody likes me, everybody hates me."*
Parent: *"Who specifically hates you?"*

This can elicit all sorts of information that is currently missing from the child's conscious understanding of the problem.

Child: *"Veronica, Stacey, Alicia and Jane wouldn't let me play with them today. They said they hate me and I am not allowed to join in."*

Now we have some specifics.

Parent: *"How do you know they hate you?"*

This will encourage the child to examine their understanding of what hate actually looks like and decide if they have really formed a well-constructed opinion.

Children, and adults, often interpret the behaviour of others incorrectly. What they currently interpret as 'hate' could easily be boundary testing, good natured teasing, insensitivity or any number of other behaviours.

The answers the child gives in this conversation will create a huge opportunity for discussion and the potential for problem solving.

Parent: *"So, you have had some trouble with friends. That is not actually everybody in your school. This happens to many children. School can be a difficult place and friendships can be hard."*

Discuss a strategy for people who do not want to play. When someone shows signs of wanting to pull away, they should be left in peace. Encourage your child to be quick to find other activities if they find themselves rejected by their peers. Often the rejection is temporary and things return to normal, however. Encourage your children to be mindful of fickle friendships.

On enquiry, you might find they believe their school friends' behaviour to be stupid and pointless. If this is the case, discuss that finding people stupid and pointless is perhaps not the best way to build good relationships. Talk about how harbouring ill feelings towards other children actually provokes rejection.

You could also explore the possibility that some children might be lacking confidence and are acting out and seeking to impress the group. Many schoolchildren have not yet figured out how to be comfortable with themselves in group situations and can easily and unwittingly make choices that can be hurtful to others. A great deal of schoolyard bullying is the result of children jockeying for position and status. Much of it is for show. The dominant child holding centre stage may not actually have the support of the group although they appear to at the time.

Being conscious of group dynamics and the bystander behaviours that occur in schools helps children to develop better resilience when they find themselves ostracised or rejected. It also serves to remind them that whether high school or primary we are talking about children, who are in general fairly socially inept and still have a great deal to learn.

Teach children to be more resilient to the meanness that they believe is present in their peer group, by being aware of different interpretations of the behaviour. Encourage them to be conscious that groups are made up of individuals who do not all think alike, and so to try to be less judgemental.

Parent: *"Is there anyone else you could play with?"*

There may well be children at school who are behaving badly or being hurtful, but there are also many children who are not.

With this comment you have turned the situation from one of discussing the behaviour of the other children to discussing the opportunities or options that exist for your child. The focus is already subtly shifting. Sometimes there is someone else in class who could do with a friend.

If there seems to be no one else to play with, discuss a strategy for finding alternate options during playtime. If reading a book under a tree sounds good, or spending time in the library drawing or writing, or throwing a ball against a wall, then make a plan that suits and works for your child. Remind them that they do not have to be accepted into all groups in school and that solitude is not the end of the world. There are times when keeping to yourself can be an okay thing to do.

Generally these difficulties are short term and your child will either re-integrate back into the group of friends with a new and improved sense of self and boundaries, or find new people to play with.

It is however important to have someone keeping an eye on things at school. A kind hearted teacher can be an extremely valuable ally, which ultimately can be all your child really needs. It could help to have a quiet word with the teacher and ask them to check that things are going okay during the break times.

Make sure that your child is aware that you are willing and able to step in if necessary but do give them the chance to sort things out for themselves if they can. Reinforce the fact that they are loved and supported at home and that issues at school are the norm and often easily turned around.

When you have devised a working strategy, do something fun together. There is no need to dwell on the problem and it makes the whole thing a lot more fun if you get a bonus play day out of it. It also puts the school experience into context. After all, school is only around 13 years of your lifespan, so it's a drop in the ocean in the scheme of things.

"Be nice to nerds.
Chances are you'll end up working for one"

Bill Gates

The Conscious Use of Language

"Outside of a dog, a book is a man's best friend.
Inside of a dog it's too dark to read"

Groucho Marx

Another tool that we can apply to the problem of bullying is to become especially conscious of the impact language has on our environment and our experience.

How we use language directly determines our experience and our outcomes, although many people are unaware of the importance of monitoring the words they use. It is equally important to be mindful of what you are willing to listen to.

Children, with their sponge-like ability to learn, are particularly vulnerable to negative language patterns and will generally form opinions about themselves based on what they hear in the home and at school.

If a child is not applying themselves to their homework, a parent, carer or teacher may, with the best intention and a desire to see the child succeed, say,

"If you don't complete your homework, you will end up a nobody and go nowhere in life."

Although the intention is to help the child, at a conscious and unconscious level they receive the *idea* that they *will not succeed* in life. This kind of thinking can stick, and if it is repeated often enough, may cause lifelong problems.

Years later you may find yourself at a loss as to why the anxious teen is feeling so terrified and desperate in the face of school-leaving exams. Fear patterns can emerge as part of that child's psyche and will become obvious when your child finds himself or herself under stress. Instilling confidence and problem-solving skills are essential to avoid being the trigger for unnecessary stress and anxiety in your child.

A more conscious choice of language could be:

> *"While you are at school, you have a fantastic opportunity to learn many things and grow in many ways, if you focus on your homework and do your best at school you will have a lifetime of benefit for the commitment you make to this moment in time."*

If your child is particularly patient and willing to listen to you then you could elaborate with:

> *"Even if you do not become the world's greatest scholar, you will learn how to apply yourself and what you are good at and what you are not so good at. School is a place where we learn about ourselves, about how to handle people, how to cope with unreasonable friendships and sometimes unreasonable teachers. It is where we learn our strengths and our weaknesses and start to see what kind of future we want to create for ourselves."*

Everything you learn in life is of value to you and every choice you make is important. School may not be everyone's cup of tea and it can be more difficult for some people to achieve high results than others, but it is a great place for you to test yourself and rise to your first challenge on the road to becoming a strong and empowered adult."

The importance here is the take-away that the child has from each discussion. In one they have installed fear and anxiety about a potential life of problems, in the other they might see a reason for committing to their own growth and development and a purpose for applying themselves to their schoolwork.

This is the single most powerful technique that a parent, friend or mentor can apply to engender more positive and healthy thinking. Paying particular attention to the use of language has profound and far-reaching implications.

Just as language can deeply embed negative thought patterns, the language we use can also cause us to remain stuck in problems. In this case a simple shift in *how* we talk to ourselves can create major life change. This example shows how you can help your child develop positive self talk:

Child: *"I am hopeless at everything, everybody thinks I am stupid."*
Parent: *"Who specifically thinks you are stupid?"*
"How do you know they think you are stupid?"
"What specifically are you hopeless at?"
"What does 'hopeless' mean?"
"Is there anything that you feel you are good at or enjoy?"

These questions, asked gently though the conversation, will draw out more information that will help the child look at solutions and provide an opportunity to discuss strategies. If they refuse to acknowledge they are good at anything, you could draw their attention to things they have done well in the past.

Another interesting language pattern could be:

Child: *"He is always angry; he doesn't like me."*
Parent: *"How do you know he doesn't like you?"*
"Have you ever been angry with someone you like?"
"Is there ever a time when he isn't angry?"

This kind of conversation will help your child create a more balanced idea of what is actually going on as opposed to the story they have currently constructed.

The language a person uses describes how they see and feel about the world. If you want to understand a person better, look at their behaviour and *how* they use words, instead of responding directly to what they say. A person who largely uses general sweeping statements like nobody, always, everybody, never, shouldn't, can't won't, has not thought deeply about what they are saying and is missing key elements. These words are indicators that further investigation is necessary.

This is not limited to children and the playground. We can all be mistaken in our thinking about a person and this can lead to confusion and conflict.

During my work as a flight attendant, I was on shift with a cabin manager who I knew no one wanted to work with. As I entered the aircraft I was greeted with her harsh barking orders and realised my trip was not going to be fun.

Some time into the flight I went down to the back of the aircraft to check on the rest of the crew. They were deep in conversation, complaining bitterly about the manager and her behaviour. Although I thoroughly agreed with their thinking, I felt the need to go and talk with her. She was making herself a drink in the galley and I quietly asked her if everything was alright as she appeared to be a little stressed. She burst into tears on the spot and told me her very sad and very traumatic story.

It was very easy for the crew, myself included, to form the opinion that she was mean and unkind. All the evidence pointed that way and we would have felt justified if we distanced ourselves and remained wary of her for the rest of the trip. We would, of course, have also created more pain and conflict for a woman who was already struggling. If I hadn't asked her the question, we may well have never understood the problem.

Each of us demonstrates our emotions differently. It is a mistake to judge another person's behaviour on face value alone, as the face they are showing you may be misleading.

Most of us could be forgiven for remaining indignant and angry with those in our life who demonstrate unsociable and unkind behaviours. It is far easier to step away and speak badly of them in secret. Sometimes, however, it is better to check.

"Love is the only force capable of transforming an enemy into friend"

Martin Luther King, Jr.

Thinking Big

"Whatever the mind can conceive and believe, it can achieve"

Napoleon Hill

If you wish to find solutions to problems, it is necessary to find common ground. This common ground is rarely found in the details of the problem, rather in a larger and more abstract frame. Linking a task with an outcome can be a great way for the unconscious mind to get on board with a project and take action. For example:

Child: *"I don't want to go to school. Everybody is mean and I don't learn anything."*

Parent: *"What do you want to do when you grow up?"*

Child: *"Be an astronaut."*

Parent: *"Ah, but to be an astronaut you need to know lots of things and many of these things you can learn at school. Is it worth learning how to handle some mean people for a little while if you are going to be able to be an astronaut one day? Perhaps you can find other people to play with or something else to do so that you don't spend so much time with the mean kids?"*

The mean children are the specifics of the problem and the lifelong dream is the larger and more abstract frame. If you and your children focus on the bigger picture when dealing with school issues, it makes it easier for you to come to an agreement about a plan. It will also help your children feel more empowered and less at the mercy of others. Keeping the outcome or goal in mind, focusing on solutions and changing perspective on the problem at hand can help both you and your child develop powerful success strategies that will be of use in many other problem situations.

If you hold the goal or outcome in mind and know that you are moving towards it, the small steps take on a much greater level of importance and you are far more likely to accomplish your objective. Sometimes we just need to get out of our own way to make things happen.

"I've come to believe that each of us has a personal calling that's as unique as a fingerprint - and that the best way to succeed is to discover what you love and then find a way to offer it to others in the form of service, working hard, and also allowing the energy of the universe to lead you"

Oprah Winfrey

Metaphors

The Two Monks

Two monks on a pilgrimage came to a river with a strong current. As they prepared to cross the river, they saw a young woman also attempting to cross. The woman asked the monks for their help.

The younger of the two monks hesitated as the members of their order were forbidden from having any physical contact with women. The younger monk turned away but the older monk gently motioned the woman onto his back and without a word proceeded to help the woman across the river. Upon reaching the opposite bank of the river, the woman thanked the monks and went on her way.

The actions of the older monk greatly troubled the younger monk, who allowed his feelings to fester. As the monks continued their journey, the younger monk became increasingly agitated and finally spoke out, "Brother, you know we are not permitted to even be in a woman's presence nor have any contact with women. How could you carry her on your back?"

The older monk looked at him and replied softly, "You are right, I did carry that woman. But I have put her down many hours ago. Why are you still carrying her?"

Zen Story

A powerful element of the tools and techniques is metaphor. Adults and children alike learn best when entertained and intrigued. Our cultural story, traditions, values, secrets, triumphs and tragedies have been passed down through the ages by word of mouth and through metaphor. A rich treasure chest of stories and metaphors is a valuable teaching tool which can transform even the direst of situations and calm troubled hearts.

Metaphors can be used as a stand-alone teaching tool without introduction or explanation. Many great spiritual teachers have depended on stories and parables to deliver their most important messages. As with humour, the value of the metaphor lies more in what has been left unsaid. If you have to explain it and break it down, it becomes too specific and loses power. In many cases the metaphor can be applied to a myriad of life situations and as such, will be of benefit to many people for many different reasons. The following stories show how this can work:

No Thank You

A Zen tale is told about the Buddha Gautama (563-483 BC), the Indian Prince and spiritual leader whose teachings founded Buddhism.

> *On an occasion when the Buddha was teaching a group of people, he found himself on the receiving end of a fierce outburst of abuse from a man who was angry that his son was being 'taken' as a monk. The Buddha listened patiently while the stranger vented his rage, and then the Buddha said to the group and to the stranger,*
>
> *"If someone gives a gift to another person, who then chooses to decline it, tell me, who would then own the gift, the giver or the person who refuses to accept the gift?"*
>
> *"The giver," said the group after a little thought. "Any fool can see that," added the angry stranger.*
>
> *"Then it follows, does it not," said the Buddha, "Whenever a person tries to abuse us, or to unload their anger on us, we can each choose to decline or to accept the abuse; whether to make it ours or not. By our personal response to the abuse from another, we can choose who owns and keeps the bad feelings."*

Be the Change

> *A woman once came to Gandhi with her son and asked if he could tell her son to give up eating sugar. Gandhi told the woman to take the boy home and bring him back the following week. One week later the woman returned, and Gandhi said to the boy, "Please give up eating sugar". The woman thanked Gandhi, and, as she turned to go, asked, "Excuse me, why did you not say those words a week ago?"*
>
> *Gandhi replied, "Because a week ago, I had not given up eating sugar".*

This story has been attributed to Mahatma Gandhi but it is possible that it predates him. It does, however, beautifully illustrate his famous quotation and overriding life philosophy *"Be the change you want to see in the world."*

Metaphors, parables and stories can be valuable, transformative and healing. They are without doubt an essential tool for teachers and mentors. Create a collection of your favourite stories and share them whenever you can. Be the change.

"A lot of people are waiting for Martin Luther King or Mahatma Gandhi to come back - but they are gone. We are it. It is up to us. It is up to you"

Marian Wright Edelman

Approaching the School

"Almost all unhappiness in life comes from the tendency to blame someone else"

Brian Tracey

If your child is experiencing bullying at school it is very important to give the teachers and/or principal an opportunity to find a solution. As a parent or carer you have a legal obligation to enrol your child in the education system and the school has a legal obligation to provide a *safe* learning environment for your child. Within this formal structure, the child's needs are greatly served when collaboration occurs between parents and educators. This helps them develop into an informed, educated and empowered person and improves their future prospects tenfold.

Tensions can run high in any school, with its mix of needs, desires, temperaments, values, rules and regulations, not to mention socio-economic, racial, cultural and religious differences. This can produce an emotional minefield of conflicting views and can make effective communication challenging.

When bullying is an issue at school, the parent or carer and the child can feel charged and reactive. Resolving these problems requires restraint and calmness along with an informed, open-minded and measured approach.

> *All children and young people have the right to accessible high-quality education free from violence, harassment and bullying. This includes any form of discrimination. Schools should provide a supportive learning environment where all students feel safe and can reach their potential. A school which allows bullying or other violent and exclusionary practices is not meeting the requirements of the Convention on the Rights of the Child.*
>
> *Violence, harassment and bullying have a negative impact on children and young people's enjoyment of the right to education. Victims of violence, harassment and bullying tend to miss school more often and achieve lower academic results than other students.*
>
> Source: www.bullying.humanrights.gov.au/children-section2

The sad truth is that some children do not feel safe at school so the onus is on parents or carers to help their child successfully navigate through. The education system includes many inspired and enthusiastic people; however, as with all bureaucratic systems faces contradictions, inequities, inefficiencies and flaws.

There are gaps in the thinking and execution of the education system, gaps in the reporting and testing procedures and gaps in behaviour management. As a consequence, there are some children who inevitably will suffer.

"The significant problems we face cannot be solved at the level of thinking we were at when we created them"

Albert Einstein

Management of bullying in school can be emotively charged and complicated. The teachers at times feel their efforts to be ineffective or thwarted by the parents of the bully. Unfortunately some parents can either be overzealous or apathetic, unwilling to participate or refuse to accept that their child may be bullying.

Schools also face the challenge of over-administration of bullying policies including programmes, documents, rationale, professional development and protocols. Sometimes the biggest issue is whether there is the ability to adopt a whole school or whole of system approach. Not all teachers, middle leaders and senior leaders are good at dealing with these issues despite a constant stream of advice and documentation. Unless all educators are doing, saying and acting from the same script then inconsistent approaches are inevitable.

State Education policy makers pressure state school principals and teachers into following protocols that may or may not be efficient or practical. Teachers who are brave enough to stray from the protocols get a rap over the knuckles and hence often retreat into a 'ignore the whole thing' phase.

Although teachers in religious and independent schools are not tied to such bureaucracy, if they get it wrong the system tends to look for the scapegoat. Some teachers would rather not deal with any of these issues as they are not trained, or they fear just getting it wrong and dealing with angry parents as well as bureaucratic jargon and protocols.

If your child is being bullied at school, there is also a chance that the school is unaware of the problem and you will have to ensure that the necessary steps are taken to resolve the problem to your satisfaction.

As a parent or carer you are your child's spokesperson, champion and at times, interpreter. Given the proliferation of behavioural problems in schools, teachers are often only able to deal with the most obvious and acute classroom issues. If you have a child who suffers in silence, then it is possible that you are going to have to agitate to produce the change that your child needs.

Schools face a mammoth task implementing behaviour management strategies. There are families for whom bullying is acceptable behaviour within the home, and their children will inevitably bring those same behaviours into the classroom and playground. If bullying is acceptable in the home it can be very difficult to address at school.

When approaching the school about potential bullying issues, bear in mind the following guidelines:

> *"I was bullied quite a lot when I was growing up in my Peking Opera School. I allowed myself to be bullied because I was scared and didn't know how to defend myself. I was bullied until I prevented a new student from being bullied. By standing up for him, I learned to stand up for myself"*
>
> Jackie Chan

1. Be calm and stick to the facts—be as objective as you can. Emotion only puts people on the defensive. Keep the heat out of the situation and focus on achieving the result you want for your child.

2. Approach the person best able to help. Generally speaking this would be your child's teacher, or if this is not suitable go to the next senior staff member.

3. Hear the other side—there may well be factors you are unaware of.

4. Be flexible and solution-focused—there may be a need for creative thinking. No two bullying cases are alike and there is not a one-size-fits-all solution.

5. Be tolerant—while your child may be hurting, remember the bully may also be facing great personal challenges. You are not in a position to judge and condemn the other child; you are there to find a solution.

6. At no point approach or contact the bully or their parents. Your job is to assist *your* child. The school is in a much better position to understand and work with the bully and their family.

7. Be solution-focused. If you fail to have your concerns addressed, find another member of staff to talk to. Keep going until you get a result. Your child is depending on you to be determined. You may need to have several meetings before you reach an agreement.

8. If the bullying has become violent, insist on action from the school to guarantee your child's safety.

9. Be willing to change schools if your child is experiencing prolonged and damaging bullying. The cost of leaving them in a hostile and crushing environment is high.

10. Be aware that if your child is struggling with bullying as an issue, there is a possibility that they will struggle in a new environment. Exhaust all possible options before choosing to remove your child.

Be mindful of getting carried away with self-righteous parental fervour. Most teachers are good people who not only have a genuine desire for children to feel happy at school but were drawn to the career because of their love of children and learning. Most have children of their own and understand what you are going through. They are *not* child psychologists and are not always well versed in confidence and self-esteem strategies.

The expectation placed on teachers to be all things to all people is unrealistic. Parents or carers need to assume the majority of the responsibility for the emotional well-being of their children and not attempt to shift the responsibility to the school.

It will help your children a great deal if you create opportunities at home for your child to discuss difficulties they may be having with peers and teachers. Once you are clear about the problem you can develop strategies, focus on solutions and work as a team.

If you are intending to handle the problem without the involvement of the school, sit with your child, discuss the options, create a workable strategy together and then give them the opportunity to step up and handle it themselves. Let them know that you will contact the school or talk to their teacher if they would like action to be taken. A great deal can happen in a single day at school and rapid turn-around from bestie to enemy and vice-versa, especially in primary years, is surprisingly common. Another option is to offer to speak to the teacher so they can be made aware of the situation but ask them not to take action. This serves as a further reassurance to your child that they are in a safe environment and that the teacher will take them seriously if they need help.

"Our age is being forcibly reminded that knowledge is no substitute for wisdom. Far and away the most important thing in human life is living it"

Frank R. Barry

Conflict Resolution Exercise

"What the superior man seeks is in himself. What the mean man seeks is in others"

Confucius

If you are in conflict with someone very close to you, you can do this exercise with that person. Go into separate rooms and write down your thoughts independently and then come together to discuss and compare notes. Set an intention before the exercise to come to a peaceful and mutually beneficial resolution.

If you are in conflict with someone that you are not close to, or do not wish to share your thoughts with, then have a close friend, parent or mentor who is familiar with the problem to work through this with you. You can also do this exercise alone although it can be beneficial to have another person's perspective. The questions below are only generic suggestions. Adapt and modify them to suit your circumstances:

1. Write down your opinion and thoughts about the person you are in conflict with. Notice if prior to the conflict emerging, you had negative feelings or thoughts about them. These thoughts and feelings can be subtle. Did you already have underlying resentment against them? If so, what was it? Did you have unreasonable expectations of the relationship? Do you feel obliged to play a role in order to please them? Do you like that role? What would you like to change?

2. Write down what you think their opinion is of you. Do they like you as you are? Do they like you only when you are aiming to please them? What do you feel their expectations of you are? What would you like to change?

3. Write down your opinion of you. Do you feel you have a voice? Do you know who you are and what you want from life? Do you feel you are able to clearly state what behaviours you accept and

what behaviours you don't accept from others? Do you believe in yourself? Do you feel yourself to be valued and valuable? What would you like to change?

If you are working with the person you are in conflict with, compare the lists and discuss them. If not, either discuss with your mentor, friend or parent or if you are working alone, spend time to contemplate the insights you have gained. Look for areas of conflict, areas of alignment and opportunities to see the conflict in a new light. Create a plan of action, implement it and move on.

"I've failed over and over and over again in my life and that is why I succeed"

Michael Jordan

Perceptual Positions

"A life lived in fear is a life half lived"

Baz Luhrmann

Another powerful conflict resolution technique for children and adults alike is Perceptual Positions. This simple process can bring an interesting perspective especially when there has been long-term conflict. This process requires a mentor, parent or facilitator to guide the person through the four steps and is easy to learn.

Place three markers on the floor, numbered one to three. These can just be pieces of paper with a number on them. Place them in a triangular fashion, at least a foot or so apart.

Position One

The 'I' Position:

Ask the person to step into position one. Ask them to fully explain the problem in detail from their point of view. Ask for all thoughts and feelings about the situation.

Position Two

The 'Other' Position:

Ask the person to step into position two, facing position one. Ask them to fully explain the problem in detail from the *other* person's point of view.

Ask "How do I think and feel about this situation and the behaviour of person at position one?" This can be an extremely valuable moment of clarity and can provide a wonderful shift in thinking. Ask pertinent questions until the topic has been exhausted.

Position Three

The 'Mentor' Position:

Ask the person to step into position three, looking at positions one and two. Ask them to imagine themselves stepping into the shoes of a trusted friend or mentor and look at the situation through their eyes. Ask how they would interpret the situation and what advice they would give to both parties.

Now the person can step back into position one. Ask some questions to help them explore the new understanding and resources they have gathered from the other two different perceptual positions.

> *Do they have any new understanding?*
> *What changes will they make to how they communicate with the other person?*
> *How will they behave differently as a result of this exercise?*
> *Have they learnt anything?*

It is important to ask them what have they learnt as it will help them to cement in a behavioural change.

This exercise can produce profound improvements in unresolved and challenging conflict.

"Those who bring sunshine into the lives of others cannot keep it from themselves."

James Matthew Barrie

Forgiveness

"Turn the pain of the past into a gain of the future"

Oxford Dictionary:
Forgive - *no longer feel angry about or wish to punish (an offence, flaw, or mistake).*

Before Wayne and I were married, the priest told us that as a married couple, in the eyes of God our previous life was over. We could now draw a line under everything that had happened in the past and be forgiven for all we had done. I had spent a great deal of my teenage years torturing myself over all the stupid mistakes I had made, the people I had let down or hurt, and the regrets that I carried with me, so this sounded like a great idea.

By looking at the definition of the word forgive, it is clear that being forgiving or unforgiving is a *feeling*, an internal letting go or a release, not necessarily an external or physical act. In order to forgive someone you do not have to actually *do* anything. It is to no longer feel angry and to give up the desire to punish. This is equally the case if you need also to forgive yourself. Letting go of resentment and anger is vital if you wish to successfully shift your focus from the problem to the solution and moving on from painful or traumatic situations.

When working with clients who have been bullied, an essential part of the coaching process is to help them release themselves from the illusion that being unforgiving has any value or purpose in life. Anger and resentment are only useful if they have a purpose and achieve a goal. Unfortunately your anger and resentment has no effect whatsoever on the bully's happiness and well-being but has hugely negative implications for you. Holding on to the pain of the past does not punish the transgressor, it punishes you and perpetuates the problem.

When you hold another accountable for their actions energetically, you bind

"You will not be punished for your anger, you will be punished by your anger"

Buddha

yourself to them until there is a resolution. This is not a good use of your energy and is not of value to you. Forgiveness ultimately is a selfish act, one that allows you to be liberated and freed from not only the past but also from the person that has wronged you.

Children usually find it quite easy to forgive, if they are taught that it is a normal and healthy practice and they understand the reasoning behind it. No good ever came from holding on to bitterness and resentment. Teaching our children to forgive easily will serve us all.

There are a couple of great tools to help with forgiveness that can be the key to turning a bullying situation around. They are intended to enlighten, to empower and to provide loving and effective guidance in moving *from bullied to brilliant*. This shift rarely happens automatically—it takes courage, action and insight. And these activities are designed to give you the tools and techniques to improve your situation.

"Holding on to anger is like grasping a hot coal with the intent of throwing it at someone else; you are the one getting burned"

Buddha

Forgiveness Meditation

"You are always free to change your mind and choose a different future, or a different past"

Richard Bach

Meditation and deep breathing are powerful and transformative practices that are imperative to learn as our connection to nature all but disappears and the pace of living escalates to a ludicrous speed.

Teaching children meditation is rewarding, vastly beneficial and will be of service to them for the rest of their days. Learning how to meditate is as essential as learning how to eat; it is food for the soul.

This meditation has its origins in the ancient Huna practices. The process has the power to heal the past, present and the future.

Remember, to forgive another is to set yourself free of the burden of carrying not only the problem but the negative connection you have to the person. Begin by listing all the people you harbour ill-will towards. Include even the most trivial of transgressions or offences—you may as well deal with all your negative energetic ties and clear the slate.

1. List each person you wish to or need to forgive. Remember to include yourself on this list.
2. Imagine an open area with a stage in the centre.
3. Stand on the stage and invite each person one at a time to come on to the stage.
4. Once the person has approached you, talk to them about what has happened. Tell them how this made you feel and what you learned about yourself from the experience.
5. Thank them for the part they played in making you a better and stronger person.
6. Forgive them for all they have done and tell them you are cutting free the negative energy tie that exists between you.

7. Ask them to forgive you for having been the vehicle and catalyst that caused them to behave badly.

8. Either hug them, or tell them that all has been put right between you and they are free to go in peace.

9. As they leave the stage, imagine the energy tie that held you to each other stretching thin and then breaking.

10. Send them blessings and let them go.

11. Repeat for each person who is on your list, including yourself.

Over the next few days, pay attention to your feelings and intuitions and write down anything that comes to you. Notice how you feel when you think about any of the people who you have forgiven. Notice if your negative feelings towards them have disappeared.

These activities can present a challenge if you believe that if you forgive you are in some way excusing or condoning the behaviour of those who hurt and bullied you. This is not the case, not remotely. Forgiveness is for you—not anyone else. For true healing to occur, it is *essential* that you forgive those who have hurt you.

Holding on to anger and resentment is consuming, exhausting and energy depleting. Forgiving people does not mean condoning their actions. Forgiveness is an act of self-preservation, healing and growth. Forgiveness is also an act of great courage, and a means of self-care. When you forgive, you open a portal to insight within yourself to improve your situation and create a healthier, happier and more creative environment for yourself and those you love.

"Pray you now, forget and forgive"

William Shakespeare

Calming Visualisation

"Think of all the beauty still left
around you and be happy"

Anne Frank

This meditation is useful for children who are feeling anxious, worried, scared or sad and need to let go of bad feelings. Use it in any situation where there has been conflict, upset, stress or trauma. It is a nice gentle way to settle a child down to sleep, however it can be used at any time. It is also very comforting if they wake with a nightmare.

This is a loose script to be modified to suit your family's beliefs and rituals.

- ❀ Tell me what is wrong.
- ❀ What feeling or feelings do you have?
- ❀ Do you want to let these feelings go?
- ❀ If you had to say where those feelings are in your body, where would they be? (Often in the stomach or chest area).
- ❀ What colour are they? (e.g. blue)
- ❀ What shape are they? (e.g. square)
- ❀ Can you close your eyes, take a deep breath and imagine the blue square moving out of your body and into your hands?
- ❀ Take the blue square now and float up high, above the house, above the clouds. Keep going higher and higher until you find yourself up amongst the stars.
- ❀ Look around for a really bright light that is for you. (Here you create whatever you wish the light to be depending on your particular faith system. You could choose an angel, a religious figure, a treasured family member who has passed or simply leave it as a light if you prefer.)
- ❀ Go close to your angel and thank them for being here for you. Ask if they will take away your bad feelings.

❀ Hand over the blue square and watch as it disintegrates into beautiful golden sparkles and disappears into the night.

❀ Thank your angel for being here for you and for taking away your bad feeling.

❀ If you have anything you want to ask of your angel, ask now.

❀ See beautiful bright light (add colours if you like) pouring in through the top of your head, filling up your body and pouring out through your feet to form a protective circle around you.

❀ Say thank you and goodbye as you slowly return to the room, bringing all that beautiful healing and protective light with you.

❀ See the light fill the bedroom and house with a glowing protective bubble and prepare for a wonderful night's sleep.

"True mastery can be gained by letting things go their own way. It can't be gained by interfering"

Lao-tzu

Mirror Affirmation

"Be not afraid of growing slowly, be afraid only of standing still"

Chinese Proverb

This affirmation is a very short, very simple and very powerful change agent that can feel rather silly when you do it; however, it is well worth the effort. If you can overcome feelings of embarrassment it is an incredibly effective confidence and self-esteem building tool.

Every morning and evening, look into your *eyes* in the mirror and say:

"I love you, I respect you and I honour the divinity within you."

You might want to write the words on a sticky note and stick it on the mirror until you have memorised them. Repeat this every morning and evening for around three minutes or until you have a shift in your feelings or make a connection to yourself. When it happens you will know what I am talking about. Do this consistently for one month.

"You are not bullied because of who you are, you are bullied because of how you see yourself"

Power Meditation

"If you add a little to a little, and then do it again,
soon that little shall be much"

Hesiod

If you are the kind of person who finds it difficult to commit to anything that remotely feels like stillness, then the five minute meditation is your answer. As an important component of a confidence and self-esteem system, the value of meditation must not be underestimated. Use this technique morning and night for six weeks. After that you will find that your day just doesn't feel the same without it. Meditation and stillness works. It changes lives.

Give yourself the gift of five minutes without focusing on the daily ins and outs of your life. This can simply be a moment to lie on your bed, or sit in a chair or in the garden. Empty your mind of *all* thought. If a thought presents itself, instead of focusing on that thought simply move it on by saying to yourself, '*I am thinking*', or '*Hello thought, thank you and goodbye*'. It will disappear.

If this still proves to be too much of a challenge, create a special place or sanctuary in your mind and go there. It could be a field, a lake, a beach, a tree, in fact whatever feels safe, inspiring and right to you. Be creative in your imagery and make it perfect for you. Be sure you are not thinking about anything else, simply focus on *being.*

Use this opportunity to invite inspiration and ideas into your life. Have a notepad and pen handy to write down anything that comes to you. Just for five minutes each morning and five minutes each night, make yourself a priority.

Secret Sanctuary

"Silence is sometimes the best answer"

Dalai Lama

I have used this tool morning and night for years and it is a transformative and energising gift to give to yourself or another. Be sure to share this technique with all you hold dear. Here is one version but the place you take yourself is yours and yours alone, so adapt this meditation to suit the pictures that appear in your mind. No one else can access your secret sanctuary, it is sacred and protected.

Picture a door, perhaps an old and worn door, or an invisible door that only appears when you touch it with your hand, it could be hidden in the bark of a tree or a rock or it could be a trapdoor covered in moss and impossible to detect. This is the gateway to your secret sanctuary and is where you go to re-energise, re-vitalise or ask for help or guidance. It is your place.

Open the door and walk through; there is a staircase inside. As you descend the staircase, notice the sensation of the steps against your feet and the appearance and texture of the walls around you. Run your hands along the handrail and see where it has been worn from all your visits. Eventually you come to another door or curtain. As you pass through you notice a soft light coming from the other side and find yourself in your secret, private and secluded sanctuary.

This sanctuary could be a beach, a forest, a field, a stream, a lake, a mountain top, a cave or any number of other places. It could be a place you remember or a place you have created, somewhere you feel safe, secure and happy.

When you are there you can do whatever you like. If you are stressed you could bathe in a deep stream or waterfall and see all your troubles wash away. You could ask for assistance or guidance, you could perhaps meet with loved ones or pets who have passed away or you could simply sit in quiet contemplation and meditate peacefully.

Whatever you choose is perfect. This place is away from the trials and tribulations of day-to-day living. Keep it clear of negative thoughts, leave your story outside and see the doorway as a protective barrier through which the difficulties you are facing cannot pass.

When it is time, leave your secret sanctuary. Pass through the door or curtain, walk up the staircase and through the second door and be sure to close them both behind you.

"I'd rather be an optimist and a fool
than a pessimist and right"

Albert Einstein

Tidy Your Sock Drawer

"Realise deeply that the present moment is all you have. Make the NOW the primary focus of your life"

Eckhart Tolle

A friend of mine who is a counsellor told me of an interesting technique she uses. Whenever she has a client contact her with depressive talk, she encourages them to clear, clean and tidy out their cupboards, garage, flat, house before taking any further action. Space clearing is a powerful agent for change. Regardless of our situation or experiences, most of us inevitably become stuck in habits, patterns and behaviours that lead us into behavioural ruts. If the rut you are in is depressing and downward spiralling, it can result in unwanted and unnecessary consequences. The act of clearing out your space acts as a pattern break and shakes up the world that you live in. This results in a flow of new perspectives and ideas. As you de-clutter your physical environment, your mental and emotional space benefits from an internal spring clean and so clears the way for new thought processes.

You must have heard the old adage, 'A change is as good as a rest'. If you are feeling down and despondent, spend some time clearing up your personal space. Throw out, sell or give away all unused and superfluous belongings and go for a walk.

You will then be able to look at how you are feeling in a more objective and balanced way.

Transforming the Bully Words

- *Natalie Hennessey*

"May we not succumb to thoughts of violence and revenge today, but rather to thoughts of mercy and compassion. We are to love our enemies that they might be returned to their right minds"

Marianne Williamson

Words can be very hurtful and harmful. Teaching your children to not take them on and to be able to transmute them is a powerful tool. Words are transient, they are not permanent and if you don't hold them, they can be let slip away.

* Gather some rocks and write the bully's words on them with washable pen. Take them to a creek or the beach and allow the water to wash them away. Then take the same rocks and write words that empower your child. You can either take them home and place them around their room or build a rock sculpture and leave it there.

* 'Write' the words using clay or plasticine, then have your child roll out the word with a rolling pin or squish it up. Next, create words that support your child.

* Use the same idea by writing the words in the sand and dancing over the top of them. Rewrite positive words.

* Write the words on paper, burn them and use the ash to fertilise a special plant you have planted for your child.

Rituals, Rites and Ceremonies for the Family - *Natalie Hennessey*

"We need to find God, and he cannot be found in noise and restlessness. God is the friend of silence. See how nature - trees, flowers, grass - grows in silence; see the stars, the moon and the sun, how they move in silence. We need silence to be able to touch souls"

Mother Theresa

Natalie Hennessey works as a special needs teacher with Queensland Education and is a *From Bullied to Brilliant* lead coach. Natalie has studied ancient shamanic practices and has a deep knowledge of ancient rites, rituals and practices.

It may not be in our conscious awareness, but all families have rites, rituals and ceremonies. While they may not be formalised or contained within a spiritual or religious context, they are more often than not tried and tested and the birth place of family traditions. In western cultures we are perhaps most familiar with ceremonies and celebrations—birthdays, Father's and Mother's Day, marriages, funerals and graduations.

Throughout history, rituals, rites and ceremonies have played a major part in the weaving of community, connection to a higher power and acknowledgement of the cycles of life—creating a tapestry of bonds, stories and memories. They are an integral part of marking and celebrating the passage of time and the effect of this on our human existence.

If you were to look at the definition of rites, rituals and ceremonies, it may give you an indication of why you would bother consciously creating any of these and why they are important still in many cultures.

❀ *Rite (of passage)—A ritual or ceremony signifying an event in a person's life indicative of a transition from one stage to another, as from adolescence to adulthood.*

❀ *Ritual—an established procedure for a religious or other rite; prescribed, established, or ceremonial acts or features collectively.*

❀ *Ceremony—a formal act or ritual, often set by custom or tradition, performed in observation of an event or anniversary.*

All are independent of and interwoven with each other. Individually and collectively they provide a platform for individuals, families, communities and countries to find common ground.

Our modern rites of passage are closely associated with our ceremonies and celebrations. Times such as graduation, engagement, marriage, birth, turning 18 or 21, death, new job or first job and buying a home are all illustrations of rites of passage that our society observes.

Family rituals can be as random and as diverse as individual families but can include such things as the Sunday family roast, Friday night football, sports day on Saturday, a television show that the whole family enjoys, sing-alongs at Christmas, or camping in the same spot every Easter holidays. Family rituals are often fiercely and loyally perpetuated because they represent great memories and the continuity of family tradition.

We all engage in these activities whether there is a deliberate consideration of their meaning and significance or not. But why do we? Is it just because we have to, because it is expected or is it for a much deeper, subconscious reason? Rites, rituals and ceremonies hold space for us to remain connected. They give expression to the unique and special energy and dynamics that are an individual family. They create a bridge between our everyday living and the sacredness of living every day. They mark the passage of time of the evolution of a family's journey.

By purposefully selecting and nurturing rites, rituals and ceremonies with your children, you will help improve their self-worth and self-esteem through a sense of acknowledgement, feeling special, supported, belonging and being valued as a member of the family and community.

Doing this does not take a lot of time, energy or money, just a little forethought and creativity. The important point to remember is there is no right or wrong way when creating your own rites, rituals or ceremonies. They just need to embrace your intention and the individual dynamics of the child and family. You can be as imaginative as you like, and involving the children with the planning and decision-making will only add wonderful experiences to share and treasure. The following suggestions will get you started.

Rituals

Creating rituals that weave a web of togetherness will add depth to family time and form the foundation for traditions and memories that can go on for generations. Be specific about the rituals you would like to adopt to foster attributes and characteristics that will support your children in becoming balanced, empathetic and strong.

- ❀ *Family homework time—having family homework time can be a special time to sit together and complete tasks for work and school. This will generate conversation and allow you to assist each other as well as making it a fun and valued time for children.*
- ❀ *Family whistle—make up a family whistle or call to use if you get separated when out in the community. This is a practical way to keep in touch and create a feeling of special togetherness, and is also a tradition that can be passed on.*
- ❀ *One to one time—schedule in regular time to spend with each of your children. It may only be half an hour, but it is half an hour that they have your sole attention and that is special to them.*
- ❀ *Bedtime routine—depending on the family personalities, this could be a time for a story (read or told), a song, or a funny routine. You could create a bedtime ritual of the child saying 'What I like about me is…'. Then you say 'What I like about me is…' Then you both take turns saying 'What I like about you is…'.*
- ❀ *Dinner routine—always try to eat together as a family without any technology. This is often the only time families connect throughout the day. Make it a time for conversation and fun. You could ask what was the best thing about the day, or what did you learn today, or how did you help today. Light a candle to symbolise your family connection. Maybe you could take it in turns to tell a joke or riddle.*
- ❀ *Once a month activity—volunteer, or spend a day in nature. Have once a month movie time or visit someone special.*

- *Sunday morning—create a Sunday morning ritual that is fun and relaxing. Perhaps it is cuddle time, or reciprocal foot massage or movie in bed.*

- *Meditation time—as a family, do some meditation. There are lots of excellent guided meditations available for kids. You could read or listen to them together.*

- *Creativity time—break out the paints, clay, instruments, dance moves, cameras or garden tools and create. Hold a family exhibition or performance or have a special display space.*

- *A special holiday tradition—this could be anything from camping, a Christmas craft or biscuit making, to leaving cryptic messages for the kids to decipher to lead them to the Easter eggs.*

- *Messages—leave loving or funny messages in their lunch boxes or under their pillows. Or find an old photo frame and put a piece of paper inside that says 'I love you because...' and enough space underneath for people to write on the glass with a whiteboard marker.*

- *Moon work—encourage your children to dream. On the full moon, release everything that is not serving them, don't want or isn't working anymore. They can just say it or write it down then bury or burn it. Then on the new moon, they can state what they want to manifest or create in the next month. This is great for acknowledging the power of thought and personal responsibility.*

Rites of Passage/Ceremonies

As well as established celebrations such as birthdays or graduations, there are so many magic moments in a child's progression that are worthy of mention. The ceremony does not have to be elaborate or involve a lot of people, just a few specially chosen ingredients that make it meaningful for all involved. The following are suggestions to get your creative juices flowing:

- *Losing the first tooth—usually for this the tooth fairy comes and leaves money, however losing the first tooth signifies they are making space for adult teeth. Why not talk about what they would like to do when they are older? It might be to travel somewhere, buy something, give to someone. Buy a special money box and put all their teeth money into there to contribute to their 'grown up' wish.*

- *Toilet training—for parents and children alike it is exciting when the potty is used for the first time. Have an 'undie' ceremony where they go with you to buy the underpants they want to use and place them in the drawer. Or buy a special step that they can help decorate to put next to the 'big' toilet so they can use it.*

- *First day of primary or high school—photos, of course! Also a new bag or lunch box that contains a note of how proud you are of them, your wishes for them or a special gift.*

- *Riding a bike—make up a photo board or video of their progression right up to the day the training wheels come off. They will love to be able to watch it when they are older. Gift them a certificate or a special something to add to the bike.*

- *Puberty—for boys and girls this is a huge transition. Take your boy camping and talk around the fire or during some physical activities about what it means to be a man. For girls it could be having a pamper or nurturing day, talking about what it is to be a woman.*

- *Menarche (first period)—ask the women in your family to buy a small gift and to write on a piece of paper or card something positive about being a woman. Take your daughter somewhere special to present her with her 'menarche box'. There are a number of very special ways to honour and celebrate this milestone.*

- *First job—if they haven't already, help them set up a bank account and/or a 'dream' fund for something they would like to purchase in the future. Place a bit of money in there to get them started and wish them luck. Depending on the work they are doing, buying them a special item of clothing, jewellery or uniform may also be appropriate and thoughtful.*

- *Getting a driver's licence—a special key ring with keys to their or the family car, or a home-made certificate stating that they can now officially drive the family car, are simple ways to acknowledge this milestone. Getting them to drive to a special place or restaurant for a celebratory dinner is another.*

- *Leaving home—have a special family dinner and present a 'home box' full of home mementos or a 'new home box' full of essentials as well as funny gifts. Buy a special key ring for their new home.*

- *Graduation—acknowledge the transition from school or university with a gift or a blessing for the future, or tickets to an event in their chosen field of work.*

❀ *Milestone birthdays—write a poem about the different stages in your child's life. Make a circle of close family and read out each paragraph from the poem (representing birth, toddler, primary school, high school). As you read, have your child walk around the circle with the other parent. Invite family members to share a memory of the child at that stage in their life. At turning 18 they could walk around the circle on their own, representing becoming an adult. Then ask everyone present to share a wish or blessings for their adult life.*

As you can see, ceremony or celebration is limited only by your imagination. Whatever you choose to do, your child will remember that special moment and the fact that you took the time to not only notice but to acknowledge it in some way.

With a child that is being bullied or has been bullied we can use rites, rituals and ceremonies to enhance and emphasise their inner strength, resilience and ability to love themselves despite others.

Natalie Hennessey
Life Coach, Mentor, Creator of Ceremony and Circle
www.spiritedwomensmovement.com

In Closing

"Wheresoever you go, go with all your heart"

Confucius

It is now time for us to bid each other adieu. As you worked your way through these pages and applied some of the tools, techniques and worksheets you will have taken yourself on a uniquely personal journey. Perhaps, as a result, you have had some interesting dreams, noticed some odd coincidences, made some chance encounters and almost certainly questioned my odd use of humour. On this journey you will have reaffirmed that you have the ability to improve your circumstances, learn new skills, change your thinking and take practical steps towards the life you dream of.

You have established that your inner world is your sanctuary, a private and unassailable sanctum and your greatest source of power to be patrolled, cared for and protected with the all the love and attention you can muster. You understand that you have complete control over your *interpretation* of life and the conclusions you draw from it. Within that single piece of knowledge lies great power and the key to happiness.

I trust that you are feeling stronger, happier and able to face the challenges that present to you in life with a big breath and an open, enthusiastic and optimistic mind.

It is my deepest desire that you understand that you are loved and loveable. It is time to tap into the limitless possibilities opening up to you right now and create a healthier, happier and more loving and creative environment for yourself and those around you.

My ultimate intention in creating this book was to help people move beyond the nightmare of bullying, perhaps smile just a little, and step into the dream of potential. If I have succeeded, even only to a degree, then I am satisfied. For now, I will leave you, my friend. Until next time…

Karen

"*Who looks outside, dreams;*
who looks inside, awakes"

Carl Jung

Alone

I saw a little fairy,
Sitting on the shelf.
I said to him are you alone?
He said no, I'm all by myself.

We fairies don't know aloneness,
For we can clearly see,
The sparkles that live inside us,
Are the same for you and me.

From Bullied to Brilliant® -The Coaching

From Bullied to Brilliant coaching system provides a radical new way to rapidly end the cycle of dominance and intimidation. Those who have been bullied will learn how to rediscover strength and purpose, find hope and self-acceptance, and move beyond bullying.

Bullying often causes you to suffer in silence and feel deeply unworthy and unimportant. Our coaches know how to help you discover exactly what prompts you to see yourself in such a negative light and more importantly, how to turn the situation around.

Through a subtle, gentle and structured coaching process you will be able to shed light and understanding on the cycle of bullying and discover how to end it. We have coaching packages for adults, students and children.

Through coaching, tasking and exercises you will understand:

- ❀ Why bullies attack
- ❀ The real problem – bullies and victims explained
- ❀ How to end the pattern of bullying
- ❀ How to turn your pain into your greatest gain
- ❀ How to let go of the past
- ❀ How to create a compelling future

Your coaches have a deep understanding of bullying and social isolation, both professionally and personally and are committed to ending the cycle of bullying, intimidation and abuse.

The *From Bullied to Brilliant* Coaching Process is a rapid and effective way to overcome and move beyond bullying.

Contact us now and schedule a complimentary 20 minute free consultation.

Contact Wayne Clarke: (+61) 0403957656
Email: admin@frombulliedtobrilliant.com
Web: www.frombulliedtobrilliant.com

Bye Bye Bully Song - Mayah :
youtu.be/5IP7HEPgd80

Resources

Abuse support services:
Lifeline
ReachOut
White Ribbon
ASCA
Safe Steps Family Violence Response Centre: 1800 015 188
Your local abuse support services

Cyber Safety Resources
www.cybersafekids.com.au
www.commonsensemedia.org
cyber-safety.com
thinkuknow.org.au
thinkuknow.co.uk
ceop.police.uk
getsafeonline.org
cyberangels.org
wiredsafety.org
http://www.pinterest.com/rtreyvaud/digital-citizenship/
fbi.gov/stats-services/publications/parent-guide
afp.gov.au/policing/cybercrime/crime-prevention.aspx
lawstuff.org.au/sa_law/topics/bullying/cyber-bullying
afp.gov.au/policing/cybercrime/~/media/afp/pdf/c/cyber-safety-top-10-tips-for-youth.ashx
afp.gov.au/policing/cybercrime/~/media/afp/pdf/c/cyber-bullying-no-crops.ashx
http://t.co/uP8zjrlTHI

Resources for Families
Parent Blog: Making Sense: http://goo.gl/ViDKRx
Reviews: Advice about age appropriate movies, books, apps, TV shows, video games, websites, and music: http://goo.gl/8iZnro
Family Tip Sheets: Age appropriate: http://goo.gl/2p95SG
Dr Phil – drphil.com/articles/article/245

On the Conscious Use of Language
Time Line Therapy and the Basis of Personality - Tad James & Wyatt Woodsmall
Magic NLP Demystified - Byron Lewis & Frank Pucelik

Recommended Reading
The Power of Now – Eckhart Tolle
Johnathan Livingston Seagull – Richard Bach
The Five Love Languages – Gary Chapman
You Can Heal Your Life – Louise L. Hay
The Element - Ken Robinson & Lou Aronica
Think and Grow Rich - Napoleon Hill
The Tao of Pooh - Benjamin Hoff
Inspired Destiny - Dr. John F. Demartini

References

Australian Human Rights Commission. (n.d.). Children and young people: key statistics and how do children and young people tend to experience violence, harassment and bullying? Retrieved from http://bullying.humanrights.gov.au/children-and-young-people-0

Australian Human Rights Commission. (n.d.). Violence, Harassment and Bullying and Homelessness. Retrieved from https://bullying.humanrights.gov.au/violence-harassment-and-bullying-and-homelessness

Australian Institute of Criminology. (2010). Covert and cyber bullying. Retrieved from http://aic.gov.au/publications/current%20series/rip/1-10/09.html

Australian Research Alliance for Children and Youth. (2009). Inquiry into the impact of violence on young Australians. Retrieved from http://www.aracy.org.au/publications-resources/command/download_file/id/134/filename/Submission_to_the_House_of_Representatives_Standing_Committee_-_Inquiry_into_the_impact_of_violence_on_young_Australians.pdf

Bullying Statistics. (n.d.). Welcome to Bullying Statistics. Retrieved from http://www.bullyingstatistics.org/

Covey, S. (2004).The 7 Habits of Highly Effective People. US: Simon and Schuster.

Cross, D., Shaw, T., Hearn, L., Epstein, M., Monks, H., Lester, L., and Thomas, L. (2009). Australian Covert Bullying Prevalence Study. Retrieved from http://docs.education.gov.au/system/files/doc/other/australian_covert_bullying_prevalence_study_executive_summary.pdf

Drummond, L. (2014). What you need to know about bullying. Retrieved from http://www.kidspot.com.au/bullying-compile/#Online and cyber bullying

Ferriss, T. (2006). The Four Hour Work Week. UK: Ebury Press.

Frankl, V. E. (2006). Man's Search for Meaning. US: Beacon.

Global Initiative to End All Corporal Punishment of Children. (n.d.). States with Full Abolition. Retrieved from endcorporalpunishment.org/pages/progress/prohib_states.html

Kamen, R. E. (Writer), Avildsen, J. G. (Director). (1984). Karate Kid [DVD]. UK: Columbia Pictures Corporation.

Lodge, J. and Baxter, J. (2012). The Longitudinal Study of Australian Children Annual Statistical Report 2012. Retrieved from http://growingupinaustralia. gov.au/pubs/asr/2012/asr2012g.html#a7.6

United Nations Human Rights. (2013). Ending corporal punishment of children. Retrieved from http://www.ohchr.org/EN/NewsEvents/Pages/ CorporalPunishment.aspx

Zocchi, M. (2012). More Sayings of the Buddha and Other Masters. Australia: Pan Macmillan.

ABOUT THE AUTHOR

Karen Clarke
From Bullied to Brilliant®

Karen Clarke is the author of '*From Bullied to Brilliant*', co-founder of 'Powerful Positive People' and a confidence and performance coach. Karen has a deep understanding of bullying and social isolation through her insight as a coach, her life-changing personal experiences of bullying, and from life in francophone West Africa. As the mother of three school-aged children, and one of seven children herself, she also understands the pressures families face when bullying becomes an issue.

Karen's book is the result of her discovery of a solution to feeling bullied, intimidated, and unworthy that works quickly and effectively. She helps parents, educators, and victims of bullying understand how a change in thinking can end the bully-victim cycle. Karen's focus is to empower people who feel helpless and give them the tools to move out of the bully-victim cycle. The world is full of questions, but our answers lie within.

www.frombulliedtobrilliant.com